Dave Silverbrand

DAVE'S HOUSE II

HOW I SURVIVED THE PANDEMIC

Dedicated to Jone Kosack,
Life Coach and Confidant

Cover photograph by Ben Anderson
Edited by Josephine Lyon

ISBN: 978-1-09837-988-9
eBook: 978-1-09837-989-6

INTRODUCTION

"What is your book about?" the NPR radio host will ask me. "About 200 pages," I will proudly reply. And so will begin my promotional tour for **Dave's House II: *How I Survived the Pandemic.***

It's all I have to show for my pandemic odyssey - this, two Moderna jabs in the arm and a couple of stimulus checks. These are the musings of a mind cluttered with life experience and from a man with way too much free time.

In the months we spent on lockdown, my life was on autopilot while my marriage nosedived. Through it all, I relived those special moments, some poignant and some funny. I rediscovered the joy of loving every one I have ever known and those I hope to meet.

This book is a celebration of life and how I spent my time, instead of ingesting bleach. I would not trade away this COVID experience. It has made me happier, deeper and more forgiving. That is why I have decided to share these stories, for better or worse.

As an Arcata transient once told my students, "I would rather be here than have Hep C." I would say the same for my own experiences, enriched through time like a festering compost pile.

Enjoy my stories. Since you have already paid for them, you might as well.

LEFT BEHIND

"Butt Paste." That is what I was thinking about the day COVID struck. As we scurried around leaving work and locking down, we pondered life in isolation - no contact with the people we loved. We would worry about food supply, toilet paper and the air we breathed. If we survived at all, we would be changing the way we lived, vulnerable to lies, speculation, conspiracies and superstition.

I worried about Butt Paste, the brown, oily ointment used for diaper rash. I had left a tube of it in my work desk as I dashed out the door. Our company had ordered us to leave the building and wait for instructions. I had grabbed notebooks, papers - all the instruments of my craft as a TV journalist. I left behind the one thing I used to treat the rash in my pants. "What if someone discovered that little red tube in my desk?" I thought. My corporate world would know that I suffered from a sore butt. My shame was unfathomable.

What embarrassment I had suffered to find that medicine. I remembered whispering to the pharmacist, the young woman in the lab coat, "I've got this burning and itching in my crotch," I said, hoping shoppers wouldn't hear me. If they did, they would tell the world that Dave's underwear was harboring strange microbes. The pharmacist ignored shoppers, advising me in a loud voice, "Try sleeping with your legs open." What good could come of that anyway? I dashed out of the pharmacy to try somewhere else.

At another pharmacy, I found an old friend. My late partner Nina had previously hired him to repair her rental houses. Projects included painting walls and plugging rat holes. His specialty was treating mold and mildew left by marijuana growers. His tools, patience and a putty knife. Now he was managing a pharmacy, harnessing his fix-up skills to human body repair.

"Try Boudreaux's Butt Paste," he recommended, pointing to the baby supply aisle. There it was - the small, red tube with the baby picture and the promise of "extra protection."

Why couldn't they have called it something more benign? "Why not 'Corpse Flower?," I wondered."

Butt Paste became the lubricant of my life. No more burning sensation at my neighborhood house fire. That's why I kept it handy with the tools of my trade - until the day the pandemic struck.

MAKING THE MOST OF THE PANDEMIC - THE PRACTICE OF POSITIVITY

There is nothing like life on lockdown to change one's view of the world. Robbed of everything we know – family gatherings, Super Bowl parties and even dining out, we are forced to become introspective. We have only the clothes on our back, the food in our pantry (when we can get it) and our own spirituality.

That spirituality has saved me. Having lost my companion of 20 years and been stricken with a life threatening heart disease, I've turned inward. I have rediscovered humor. Those motorized supermarket carts are no longer crutches - but rather fuel-injected race cars.

I gleefully rediscovered my own story while reconnecting with my older brother Peter, a former race car driver. He is now an inmate suffering from terminal cancer. I have also found order in chaos. I thank God for the people who hurt me and hate me, as well as those who love. This is my story from the recycle bin of my mind.

MY WORRY LIST

I adored my childlike qualities. Nobody else saw the world the way I did. As it grappled with a deadly virus, I worried about the rash in my shorts. I wondered existentially. Why do fleas turn back-flips when they jump? How did they communicate and what would they say to each other? These were nagging questions to which my mother always had the same answer: "It's God's will."

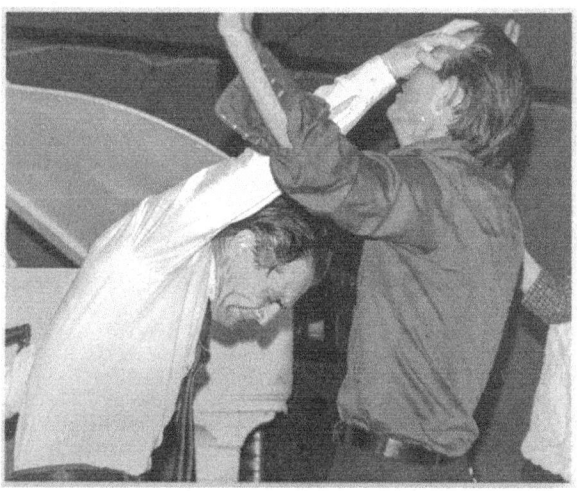

My early days as a Silverbrand with mother, Elizabeth, father Edmund and brother Peter. My first words were, "Isn't that nice."

I had always seen the world through a toddler's optimism. "Isn't that nice?" were my first recorded words. And for the rest of my adult life, I would assume that everything was "nice" until it was proven otherwise.

"Bambi," fit that narrative. It was the story of fluffy, cute animals gamboling in the forest spouting words to live by. "If you can't say something nice, don't say nothing at all," Thumper the rabbit advised his forest friends.

How cruelly Walt Disney had shattered my bliss. I remember watching the movie as a five-year-old, my mother holding my hand. Then, I heard the rifle shot, Bambi's mother killed by a hunter. "Man has come to the forest," said the animals, and I screamed in horror. For years to come, I would imagine my world as an idyllic place, impervious to evil. But if anything, Bambi should have prepared me for life's reality - humans can be cold blooded.

As a 12-year-old with my own bedroom, I had decided to be a foster dad to two white mice. The boy who had them said they were the same gender. Therefore, there was no need to separate them, I thought.

Of course the boy was wrong: one was male and the other female. Quickly, my two mice became eight, the parents and six little tykes scampering under my bed and depositing droppings everywhere. What a harsh way to learn about unplanned pregnancy. My parents hadn't prepared me for this - but then, they weren't prepared for the Silverbrand boys either.

My older brother, Peter, was smart but calculating. He knew how to have fun with dangerous things - firearms and explosives. While I was celebrating life through my mice, he could put life in jeopardy. I believed in paying it forward. He preferred payback, resolving conflict by having the last word.

When his school principal decided to punish him for bad behavior, Peter had an ax to grind. The principal was our father, Edmund. Peter knew how the cookie crumbled - or, in this case, the whole cake.

Banished to the corner of the principal's office, 11-year-old Peter asked if he could eat his lunch. Then, unwrapping his chocolate cake, he allowed its crumbs to fall to the floor. None of the cake made it to his mouth. So, at the end of his half-hour punishment, Peter had sifted a mountain of chocolate crumbs.

At the time, I was amused by his cunning. He invented buttons to mute our television commercials and buzzers to announce our visitors. He was the envy of our father and confidante to our mother. He could reassemble an engine from memory and commiserate with our mother when she needed comfort.

Later, he took an interest in my radio jobs, visiting the places I worked just as I would watch him race cars. Once, Peter placed second in a big Santa Barbara sports car race. Our father wrote a press release about it, giving it to the Manager of the station where I worked reading the news. When I finished the news that Monday, the dee-jay questioned me on the air about the press release I didn't read about my brother.

"Are you ashamed of your brother?" ask the announcer.

"No," I answered sheepishly.

"Well, read it then," he demanded.

Reluctantly, I did, mouthing my father's words: "Silverbrand, known affectionately to his friends as 'Pete' was driving a yellow MGA rebuilt in the family's garage."

Of course I was proud of my brother, but as a budding journalist, I was also wary of being too close to a story. I wanted to be objective and independent. I didn't like being told what to read. On the other hand, if Peter had asked me to read it, I would have done that. That was the measure of my respect for him.

SOUTH OF THE BORDER

Perhaps Peter was restless with the idyllic life we led. We lived in a farmhouse next to a walnut orchard, it had all the trappings of a quiet country life. For Peter, things were just too quiet and he constantly looked for excitement. He found it in Mexico. When he began traveling there for marijuana smuggling, he was sure to run afoul of people on both sides of the law.

Planning a weekend in Tijuana, Peter asked to borrow my prized possession, a wooden model of a Thompson sub machine gun I had bought as a kit. The life sized machine gun could pass for real firepower, especially in the dark. I asked him why he needed it and he said he wanted to "settle a score." I can only speculate what that meant. Burned by a drug dealer, Peter would brandish the firearm and scare him. Naturally, a stunt like that these days would be fatal. His adversary would respond with live ammo and Peter would be buried outside town. We grew up in innocent times.

He lost his freedom through the wrong people. He knew a man alleged to have imported illegal automatic firearms from Vietnam. According to Peter, federal investigators were zeroing in on the Californian, presenting evidence to a Grand Jury. Peter also knew the man who would be witness to that grand jury, also a friend of the importer. When the informant was shot dead on his front porch, police began to suspect Peter... The van the killer used was registered to Peter. He also made gun silencers and studied assassination techniques and had books on assassination. He kept his tools in the bedroom of our mother's in Visalia. He could not account for his whereabouts the night of the killing.

A Placer County Superior Court convicted him of murder while lying in wait. A judge sentenced him to life without parole. Through the years, I wrote to him and spoke daily by telephone. We were, after all, the Silverbrand's, for better or worse.

OTHERING

As the Silverbrand brothers, we didn't always get along. Our younger brother felt he was the entitled one. When our Aunt Virginia chose me as ring bearer for her wedding, she gave me a toy car as compensation. My younger brother burst into tears, insisting that he wanted a toy car too. She bought him one, forever teaching him that he could always hijack our happiness. He found that the best way to do that was to be miserable and marginalize joyful people like me. Social scientists have a name for it now, "othering." My younger brother was an expert at "othering" me throughout our childhood, a practice he still follows.

It was easier in our sheltered home where, as children, we learned to create our own reality. Mine was an imaginative childhood in which I was Hopalong Cassidy, Roy Rogers and Zorro. I enjoyed detective work the most. Our farmhouse outside Oxnard was a hotbed of crime, stray dogs and missing newspapers. Dogs were recidivists. You could chew one out for peeing on your lawn and when his bladder refilled, he would be at it again. They were scofflaws, seeming to know how to be annoying without being captured.

I was more suited for investigating undelivered newspapers. With plaster, a tape measure and a ring of skeleton keys, I would stake out the newspaper drop-box, keeping vigil for paper thieves. With the plaster and tape measure, I could preserve and measure tire tracks. The skeleton keys served no useful purpose. They just sounded great hanging on my belt. In my months as a private detective, I would never crack a case. But sometimes the deterrent was enough, and nobody messed with the kid with the skeleton keys.

I avoided family outings because they were too real. I preferred staying at home, free to play in my happy world. When I outgrew detective work, I moved on to deejay on my father's stereo. With the family gone on Sunday drives, I would produce record shows complete with commercials and newscasts. I first discovered my affinity for deejaying when neighbor kids would play baseball in the street. I would open the living room window and play Spike Jones records at full volume. I don't know if the kids were paying attention; but, I learned that it didn't matter. That was the miracle of broadcasting - just put out your product and then don't think about it. I didn't have to worry about relating to an audience. I just wanted to create and then be left alone.

My younger brother did not like that about me. He liked to tease me, sometimes maliciously. When he discovered that I was horrified by a caterpillar photo in a nature book, he chased me around the house with it. There was something chilling about the two green creatures with bulging eyes slithering toward me. It reminded me of the 1932 black-and-white horror movie "Freak Show." In the Tod Browning film, real circus sideshow performers overpower an evil man by trapping him beneath a wagon. The last haunting scene of the movie shows performers crawling toward him through pools of mud. Over time, my younger brother would use that tactic more often.

BEGINNING JOURNALIST

I got journalism fever in the fifth grade. That's when I decided to publish my own newspaper, *The Oxnard Courier*. Sunday afternoons, I would hand-print my edition on duplicating paper, the kind teachers would use to make classroom assignments. I would glean information from Oxnard's daily paper and also write observations about interesting things I saw on family outings.

One such story described an old Black man poised at the entrance to Oxnard's Wagon Wheel Restaurant. Dressed in chef's garb, he would wave at passers-by, like me. I felt a personal connection and hand-printed my story about him. "Maybe you have seen the old man outside town waving to people," my story began. It would end when I ran out of space.

Then, I would cajole my father to print copies of the paper on the school duplicator for publication the next day at school. I would charge two cents a copy, a bargain compared to the 35-cent Los Angeles Times. My first publication day did not go well. Selling the paper to students lined up before school, I must have irritated one. For no reason, he punched me in the stomach, a solid smack I can still feel. For that, my younger brother was reprimanded by our teacher. I learned early that bullying of reporters could happen at any time. I abandoned my newspaper project, but not my interest in journalism.

In time, I would be attracted to radio journalism. There in the studio, I had at least one layer of protection, the building itself. In high school, a teacher recognized the journalist in me. Or, maybe he was simply trying to keep my attention. Ralph Rothrock, my Sophomore English teacher, told me that a local radio station, KNEZ the Breezy 960, needed someone to report on local city council meetings. He suggested that I attend one and write a news script. I was fascinated by the public meeting, finding old men, stammering and joking through their policy-making process. It reminded me of school study hall, governance at its worst. I wrote a two-page account of my experience. Nothing ever came of the project. Still, I never forgot the experience because I was awakened to a new concept in writing. Apparently I was onto something because by the time I was in college, Lompoc folks were tossing the old politicians out of office. It was the subject of my Political Science term paper, The Lompoc Recall Election. College was no place for a young man with a short attention span.

Peter had the same problem, flunking out of college where he majored in Automotive Technology. He preferred to fly model airplanes. I was fueled by the adrenaline of life experience. My journey to puberty was a rugged Southwest Passage threatened by sidewinders and Gila monsters, shyness and fear of rejection. I learned life lessons by making mistakes, baring my teeth to the biting desert wind, my eyes burning from the boiling water pump of my broken heart.

In truth, the automotive radiator became the crucible of my transition to manhood. It signaled the last time my brothers and I faced adversity together. We were never the same after the night a radiator gave out - the night I became a man, fighting back the tears of a child in a cloud of hot chili pepper. It was the night the black holes of the universe were no match for the one in our engine compartment.

THE PEPPERED RADIATOR

It happened on a drive back from Riverside to Lompoc, a seven hour trek. My brothers and I had taken the old family Pontiac Sedan, a 1950 Chieftain, to an auto race south of Los Angeles. On the Sunday night drive home, its engine overheated and we stopped for help at a South Central Los Angeles gas station. It was in a Latino neighborhood where the mechanic recommended pepper to plug the radiator hole. He said pepper would settle on the leak giving us time to get home. At a small market next door, we bought jars of chili-peppers, Peter dumping them strand by strand into the radiator. Then, he filled the radiator with water and we headed north, extra water stored in empty oil cans.

The overheating didn't stop. Boiling radiator water cooked the peppers, filling the car with an eye burning mist, a Jalapeño Hell. Peter could barely see to drive and I stuck my head out the open window as we wept and gasped. Just before dawn, our peppered Pontiac gurgled its way down the driveway to our Lompoc house and we stumbled to bed. It wasn't easy the next morning explaining to the high school attendance officer why I wouldn't be coming to school. How could I explain that I lost my sense of smell?

For years, my brothers and I have wondered about the pepper treatment. "Maybe the mechanic was having fun at our expense," I thought. For the life of the car, its upholstery carried the scent of burnt tamales.

Forty years later, I learned that the chili treatment was legitimate. We had just misunderstood details. According to a radiator repair mechanic, *powdered* pepper could plug leaking radiators. The powder would settle on the leaks, plugging them until the radiator was fixed. That was our mistake. The Los Angeles mechanic had recommended pepper powder while we used whole peppers. In other words, we had been pepper sprayed by our own stupidity, falsely blaming an entire culture.

LOVE ON THE PLAYGROUND

In the eighth grade, hot blood flowed through me like a hot pepper in a Pontiac. Girls were all I thought about, their popping bubblegum stirring my soul. On the last day of junior high school, couples gathered on the playground to bid farewell, the 8th graders heading off to high school combat. They would write, of course, as they hunkered down in the foxholes of "Detention." The junior high schoolers began to kiss goodbyes as they swallowed their gum.

Word spread among underclassmen that something wild was unfolding on the playground. They dashed down the hallway to see and smooch. Horrified teachers blew whistles as they raced to the basketball courts. "Stop!" yelled one as the kissing continued. Clearly, the genie was out of the bottle. We had seen primal love, not through Sandra Dee and Bobby Darin, but through classmates, braces and all. We would never be the same.

Until then, most of what I knew about sex I learned through *Catcher in the Rye*, the J.D. Salinger book my father had forbidden me to read. He believed that the coming-of-age novel about Holden Caulfield was much too graphic - the reason I read it. Until then, the Sears catalog was the center of my reading regimen. The Fall and

Winter Edition always featured full color photos of beautiful women in baby-doll pajamas and underwear. The Spring and Summer Edition added swimwear.

My mother must have been the first to notice those worn catalogs on the bathroom reading stand. My brothers never talked about relationships except in cynical terms. In high school, neither had a girlfriend, dismissing girls as a distraction from the more relevant model airplanes and fireworks.

One day, Mom bought me a book about puberty and changes to the body. It explained my fixation on Vicky, the young clarinetist in our band. I eyed her across the woodwind section and followed her on the way home from school. Once I asked her for a date, though I never explained where or when. Her saying "Yes" was all I needed. In the meantime, my fantasy world revolved about Saturday night movies at the Lompoc Theater. There I would swoon over Debbie Reynolds as Tammy, the Bayou girl with the big bra.

Meanwhile, the girls were swooning over anyone with a British accent. It started with the Beatles, of course, but within months, every other English pop group had a chance of making a splash in America.

One of the was *Peter and Gordon*, an English duo rising to fame in the 1960's. When they announced a concert in Santa Maria, it was a big deal. They were as close to famous as we would get.

I dug out my KNEZ blazer and borrowed a small tape-recorder for a backstage interview after the show. I typed out my questions in advance so I could present myself as a savvy music reporter. Back in the dressing room, I nervously turned on my recorder and began reeling off my questions: "What do you think the current trends in music are towards?"

They didn't understand the question any more than I did and they mumbled something impatiently as my tape-spool gathered the sound recording. I couldn't wait to put it on the air, proving to our Lompoc listeners that I was becoming a force in the music business.

At home, I anxiously turned on my machine to hear the great interview. There was nothing there. I had failed to turn up the recording volume, the sound forever lost in oblivion.

It crushed me. No record of my interview with famous recording stars, nothing of a back and white photo of my big chance for music fame, a tape with nothing but the hissing sound my worthless machine.

With recording stars Peter and Gordon at a Santa Maria concert. I'm the one who is smiling.

RARIFIED AIR

If my love life had been a Dodger game, Vin Scully would have described my plate appearance as "a little nubber off the end of the bat." My time with Wendy, a community college classmate, was equally disappointing. First, I tried a romantic picnic in the park. With a basket of sandwiches and my guitar, I took her to a shady grove. After lunch and light conversation, she asked me to play my guitar. "Oh I don't play," I responded. "I just brought it for effect."

My tool of romance, the guitar I would bring on dates to the park. Of course, I couldn't play a note with it. I just used it for atmosphere.

In my red MGA, I took her out one more time to a romantic Lompoc restaurant. I was sure that was the night for my big "move." I assumed that a good tri-tip steak had to be worth something in return.

On the way home, we stopped at Lompoc's scenic overlook. From there we could see the lights of the city below. The universe was in full display, from the Big Dipper in the sky to the Lompoc home of the chocolate dip, Fosters Freeze, on Main Street. I told her that at 1000 feet above sea level, the air was thin, putting her life in peril. That's when I leaned over to her saying. "You might need some mouth-to-mouth resuscitation." "No, thank you," Wendy replied distantly. Striking out swinging, I sullenly drove her home and left without a word. I didn't see her again after that. I'll bet she became a respiratory therapist. I hoped I would fare better in love's big leagues, San Jose State University.

An hour's drive from San Francisco, it was witness to the Summer of Love. We could dream of life with hillside hedonists but in my dormitory, we had to settle for something less. Our good time was under the command of Colonel Sanders, a bucket of chicken and a night sharing love stories. We all had many sexual encounters to recall, most of them fictional.

Without a story to tell, I would stroll from the men's dorm to the women's dorm. There by the hour, I could watch couples kiss and imagine myself among them. I won my first college kiss at a carnival wheel of fortune. At a fraternity fundraiser, I had spun the wheel for a chocolate bar but it stopped on the sorority smooch. What followed was a kiss for the ages. If nothing else, it fueled my appetite for more.

WHERE IN THE WORLD IS CHARLES?

I had always been inspired by free spirited people, among them, fellow Journalism student, Charles. It took courage to pass out drunk as he did on the floor of the prestigious San Francisco Press Club. The city's venerable writers were forced to step over his body as they left the club that night.

His unique view on life was not limited to the Press Club ceiling. It was reflected in his folksy writing style. For his college newspaper, he wrote, "Miss Swanson is in the hospital this week having been [sic] bitten by a spider in a bathing suit." I wanted to know what kind of bathing suit a spider would wear. As a San Jose State Spartan writer, Charles was a Grecian warrior achieving mythological status.

The kitten story was one example. In Greek mythology, a Spartan child had hidden a fox under his coat as he studied. So focused was he, he allowed the fox to eat out his stomach rather than cease his studies. He died a hero with a scholastic "incomplete." He just didn't have the stomach for it. Charles had that same sense of destiny. Under his shirt, he smuggled a kitten into his newspaper class. On that hot, humid day, the kitten grew tired of captivity, the sweaty belly of the beast. He bit into soft flesh as Charles screamed in pain. Once again, Charles had earned his legendary status.

Maybe that was the day Charles decided that academic life was too much for him. A month before graduation, he went to San Francisco to become a "Flower Child." He apparently had no plan to return to class. If only he had sought a psychologist in the college's "Building K." In a 1967 edition of the paper, a student reporter wrote, "Building K" offers a secure atmosphere where they can talk out their problems. (It) differs from a mental institution where people are cut off from society."

I had personally used "Building K" to address my shyness. I told the counselor that a girlfriend had sex with me and I wore no condom. He insisted on going with me to a drugstore to buy some, a case of the "rubber" meets the road. It was the height of the "Summer of Love", when San Francisco undulated with the energy of the Flower Power Generation. Often, I would drive alone to the city, parking my car near the Haight-Ashbury District. I would walk its streets, watching young people caught up in the celebration and the drugs. "Acid?" someone would whisper as he passed by. He was selling LSD, the best way he knew how, announcing that he was "holding," To the sound of bongo drums, I would pass the afternoon observing the pageantry.

Charles' disappearance added a sense of urgency to my mission. With a small search party of other students, I walked the streets, showing a snapshot of my classmate. "Have you seen this guy?" I would ask. One had. "Oh, that's Tiny," he said, recognizing that Charles often walked the streets selling editions of the "Berkeley Barb," the underground paper about street life. Now, our missing friend had a nickname, another way to find him and bring him home. That was as far as we got. A competent investigator would have asked the paper to publish the photo of "Tiny." We gave up and headed back to San Jose.

We never heard from Charles again. My guess is that somewhere in the Midwest, he is writing birth announcements for a small weekly newspaper, an angry kitten stashed under his shirt.

Learning my craft at San Jose State University. Learning how to edit 16 mm film. I assumed that once my acne cleared up, this skill alone would have me working in the biggest TV stations in the country.

RETURN TO HAIGHT-ASHBURY

Years later, I would return to the neighborhood where Charles disappeared. It was inhabited by other men with similar stories. One was Pete the Poet, drinking beer and eating noodles on a bench. Every poem began, "Purple Haze swirling around my brain...", and ended unintelligibly. He took me to a garage where Jimmi Hendrix had once rehearsed and Janis Joplin's apartment. Pete told me that he too had lived in Visalia and gone to San Jose State College. What happened to him after that was anybody's guess, forever lost in the haze just as Charles was. I offered to buy Pete a 6-pack of beer but he wanted only one.

Down the street, a middle-aged couple sat in the sun and talked about the evolution of their neighborhood. Once, children were frightened by naked people running through the streets, they told me. Now they felt a sense of order. He had married the mother of three, spending their wedding night in an abandoned library. Friends had barricaded the building with shopping carts so the couple could have privacy.

Maybe Charles belonged there after all, along with Pete the Poet and the couple, enjoying life in love. Maybe we were the ones left behind.

SUMMER IN EUROPE

That graduation summer, 1968, I got another chance to grow up. A student friend was going to Europe for the summer and invited me along. Donald Cox and I were flying to London, two ducklings off to see the world. Except on family camping trips, I had never been out of California. I was about to deal with Britain, where people drove on the left. If I had asked, I would have learned that the practice dated back to the Middle Ages when people traveled by horse. If the passing rider meant harm, one would have a free right hand for a sword. I would soon learn about the other differences between primates who walked, dressed and behaved differently from small town Californians. For one thing, they loved the dark ale that upset my stomach. We also learned that Australians never quietly go to bed. Every beer-fueled night ended in fits of dementia. In a rooming house where we stayed our second night, Aussies burst through the door, overturning our beds and laughing hysterically. I chronicled it all in a handwritten journal.

We had spent our first evening at a London pub, Prospect of Whitby's. We had begun our quest for European lovers, hoping that our California swagger would attract women. We were wrong, of course, a point painfully obvious in our 10 weeks on the Continent. Two homely men with "Europe on 5 Dollars a Day" travel guides were simply lost souls - hungry and whiny. Donald schooled me in the significance of the Mona Lisa, the Sistine Chapel and Rome's Coliseum while I complained about the language barrier, the heat and lack of sleep. I also complained about Eastern Europe travel restrictions and waiting in line. When we tried to buy train tickets from Prague, Czechoslovakia to East Berlin, I was told by the ticket agent that I would need a transit visa. "I just want to leave your country," I whined in frustration. "At least you can leave," said the agent. I had so much to learn about the world.

But that didn't stop me from trying to pass myself off as a "foreign correspondent." I filed a "dispatch," about my Eastern Europe observations to my hometown newspaper, The Visalia Times-Delta. Surely with all their small town gossip and meaningless minutiae, I thought, the paper would be interested in a hometown boy on the Cold War front. They were not. Rejecting my article, the editor sent me an unapologetic rejection letter. What did he know beyond the price of Visalia walnuts? While he was pounding an old Underwood typewriter, I was dipping my toes in Rome's Trevi Fountain. And what did I know about fountains? Nobody told me it was against Rome to wash my feet in them. If busty Anita Ekberg could do it in "La Dolce Vita," why couldn't I? If only the world could meet my expectations.

Nothing humbles the world traveler like coming home to people who didn't miss me. My mother was the only one. I stayed with her for the rest of that summer. As mothers do, she worried about the weight I had lost and vowed to fatten me up with fresh biscuits. The rest of my family paid little note - each self-absorbed. For my brother Peter, drug smuggling was in high gear with his frequent marijuana trips to Mexico. Then he would drive his sales route through Berkeley and San Francisco. He would make a final swing back to Lompoc where he lived in the family-owned home. My father was rediscovering his youth, carrying on an extra-marital affair with a school secretary. He was terrible at subterfuge, meeting his lover at a popular motel. Mom would send me on scouting missions, cruising along Mooney Boulevard, Visalia's "Sunset Strip."

LIVE FROM LOMPOC

"An informed citizen is the cornerstone of democracy," came the recorded voice at the end of the KNEZ newscast. With a drum roll, they all ended that way as the local dee-jay segued to the next record: "And the hits just keep on comin'." One old dee-jay I knew preferred a more stately introduction: "And the curtain rises on our mythical stage revealing a vast galaxy of recording stars." Mick Jagger would then follow with, "What a drag it is getting up." That was the opening line to *"Mother's Little Helper."*

I always had a flare for English dating back to my formative years in Lompoc radio. I had been assigned to broadcast the city's Flower Festival Parade, a celebration of the city's seed industry. Our station could not afford the usual broadcast line from the parade. The afternoon announcer, Hank Seegar, gave me a handful of dimes and told me to find a telephone booth. From there I could telephone reports in the great Edward R. Murrow tradition. I did so with flair, announcing "Here comes a band. There goes a horse." Periodically, the operator would intercede with, "Please deposit a dime for another three minutes."

As Dave "Tune-Decks" Sherwood, I would play the hits on KNEZ, *"The Breezy 960."* We called them the *"Boss 40,"* the hottest songs on our playlist. We called the new songs our *"Picks to Click,"* or "Waxes to Watch," although I have no idea what those phrases meant.

The next year, I broadcast the parade from the front office of the downtown studio. I had learned to embellish my accounts, calling the passing horse a "gelding stud." "There is no such thing as a gelding stud," my boss advised me. "The horse is either a gelding or a stud. It can't be both," he told me. I would have asked why but I knew it was way over my head. On a visit back to the old radio station years later, I found it had switched ownership and purpose. It was a locksmith and gun shop operated by a dour man. He rejected my suggestion for a new business name, *"Locks and Glocks."* A taxidermist I met had a similar reaction. I told him to call his shop *"Stuff This."* As an old boss once told me, "You think you're funny but you are only fooling yourself."

Everything I knew about sleepy Lompoc had changed. A haven for street gangs, it acquired the nickname *"Compton-North."* The flower market moved overseas and business people considered conversion to a cannabis-based economy. That came 50 years too late for my younger brother, busted for growing a single plant in our basement. In the 1960s when that happened, it was front page news as police posed with their evidence haul, a half-dozen marijuana plants. My school principal-father was embarrassed by the bust, our family name listed in the news article. As Silverbrand's, we had a knack for attention along with a healthy file of police reports. For me, moving away from home didn't come soon enough.

When I returned for a visit once, my father seized on the opportunity to belittle me, "I see you're still trying to grow a mustache," he said. Maybe that was the genesis of my beard-shaving collection. During our pandemic, I I developed an odd collection of keepsakes, among them my electric razor shavings. I would empty the contents of my shaver, flakes of skin and specks of hair, into a medicine bottle. I couldn't understand the reason, nor impress anyone with them.

I could have chosen instead to collect the wax from my ears. Periodically, it would thunder around my inner-ear canal before dropping to the floor. That process too fascinated me and inspired many hourse of research.

FORCE-FED MATURITY

As a college graduate, I knew I needed to grow up. That is why, in 1968, I left my California home to be a VISTA Volunteer. Ads about the Johnson Era "War on Poverty" described VISTA as a campaign to rescue the poor. "If you are not part of the solution," they proclaimed, "You're part of the problem." It was never made clear to me what my specific talents could do to help anybody. I was a blank slate, void of practical survival skills. I was Bambi, the Disney fawn wandering in the forest.

My VISTA colleagues were just as naive. Two young musicians believed that a brass band would be the instrument of change in the ghetto. They proposed instruments to would-be gang members. I envisioned them taking their clarinets and piccolos to the city's mean streets, a remake of "The Music Man." But urban gunfire was a far cry from "Trouble, right here in River City." It outgunned Professor Harold Hill and Marian, the Madam Librarian. It also proved no match for my VISTA friends who moved to the inner city, New Haven and then disappeared.

I decided to be a novelist in the manner of Ernest Hemingway. He would live his tales. I felt I had that opportunity in New York, alive with pathos. I would walk the streets alone, not distracted by the other VISTA Volunteers. I approached a young hooker on a Brooklyn street corner and asked her fee structure. "You wanna date, Honey?" she replied.

"Just price checking," I responded. "Twenty dollars." "I'll get back to you," I replied, jotting the figure on my notepad. I didn't follow through, of course. I had my limits.

A writing teacher had once told me to write only about what I knew. And as a tenderfoot from Visalia, I didn't know much. That street life price check was the first time I had asked a question about anything. The federal government would send us to communities to organize the poor people, failing to tell us what the poor were to do. That was left to us, privileged dreamers, to give them direction. We were simply upper-middle class white folks dodging the draft.

I wrote chirpy articles for a neighborhood newsletter and letters to the editor for the weekly paper. In one, I responded to a war veteran who complained that people at the Memorial Day parade would not salute the American flag as it passed by. I responded that the flag was only a piece of cloth, a superficial symbol. That letter got me a reprimand from our boss who told me to mind my own business. It was not a good idea to dress down a veteran at the taxpayer's expense. Accordingly, I kept a low profile by golfing at a local course, parking my federal car for all to see.

The draft lottery of 1969 changed everything. That was the national numbers game selecting probable draftees by birthday. I got a high number, meaning I wouldn't be drafted. Essentially, that ended my VISTA dedication. I became News Director at WINY Putnam, Connecticut radio station. There I nearly set the world on fire or - more to the point - the radio station itself. I left a smoldering coffee coil near a pile of news scripts. My boss caught it minutes away from full ignition.

With my portable tape recorder, I would dash from one public meeting to another, putting stories with sound bites on the morning news. It was groundbreaking, the Putnam mayor objecting to my recording meetings because of his French accent. I loved covering breaking news, dashing to the scene with my recorder at my side. There was nothing more compelling than the sound of a car fire on the interstate. As a radio news reporter, I was always frustrated by its limitations – no pictures. Years later, for KHSU Public Radio, I covered a new police drug detection dog at the California Highway Patrol. For a full half-hour, I recorded the sound of the CHP extolling the dog's virtues while the German Shepherd lounged in the sun. It made for a boring radio story. Then, stepping back, I dug my heel into the dog's tail. He jumped to his feet snarling, threatening to take me down. I would have done the same. The dog was the only "soundbite" worth airing.

Public radio listeners frequently questioned my news judgment, especially airing the verdict in the O.J. Simpson murder trial. One Petrolia listener wondered why I couldn't have covered the whale migration instead. I thought he should stop "blubbering."

A JOURNALIST BLOSSOMS

Put an infinite number of monkeys in a room full of typewriters and they will type all of Shakespeare's plays. In my first radio news gig, a drunken monkey could have done my job. It wasn't my fault. I lived in a sleepy little mill town with no news. Nothing ever happened that required an active verb. My own newscasts were so boring that I fell asleep in the middle of them. The announcer taught me to tap my foot as I read the news to keep myself awake. For that I earned $140 a week. I would have made that at the thread mill. My big story was the local election in which Republicans won every office. Democrats alleged fraud, dead people voting. In comatose Putnam, you couldn't tell the difference.

I longed for the "big show," TV news and got my chance in Aroostook County, Maine, the heart of potato country - a heart with blocked arteries. Nothing but snow happened there. Two candidates applied for the anchor job and because I did not stutter, I got it, making $120 a week. With a U-Haul trailer, I headed up the Maine Turnpike. My apartment there was a basement storage room with no windows, perfect for a family of gophers. I would share the toilet with office workers upstairs and bathe at the landlady's house across town. I would fall asleep to the serenade of big rigs idling outside. Their drivers kept them running so they wouldn't freeze. Presque Isle had been home to my great-grandfather, Franklyn Sumner Sprague, a potato farmer, bear hunter and storyteller. His bear stories were suspect because no one ever saw his game. I was carrying on the family storytelling tradition. My hour-long newscast featured cooking tips and potato market prices.

Our station manager spent his time crying in his office. Once again, I creatively caught fire, nearly incinerating the floor at a big, local banquet. The Chamber of Commerce had assembled Potato Blossom Queen candidates. I was sent to film young ladies in their evening gowns. The incident happened during my filming. I set my spotlight down - still burning - to wind up the spring on my news camera. The hot spotlight melted the vinyl tile, sending a mushroom cloud of acrid smoke to the ceiling. As young women dashed out for air, I slipped out the backdoor. They would never know the smoke source, only that some evil spirit had visited upon them. Maybe they needed that to ensure their virtue. Assuming responsibility for the fire would not have solved anything.

Besides, I was headed to a big new job in Portland. There I became a feature reporter, describing unique, local people. They included a boardwalk weight guesser, a pun-addicted school teacher and a faith-healer. Since the faith healer was supported by a portable generator, my spotlight had a spiritual impact on his tent revival. It made the lights dim and lowered the organ pitch by a half step.

Reverend James Reynolds was a Pentecostal preacher, pitching his revival tent in Portland's city park. There on those warm summer nights, he would preach the Gospel, beginning in low measured tones. But soon, he would be raising his voice as he told Bible stories of faith and triumph over evil.

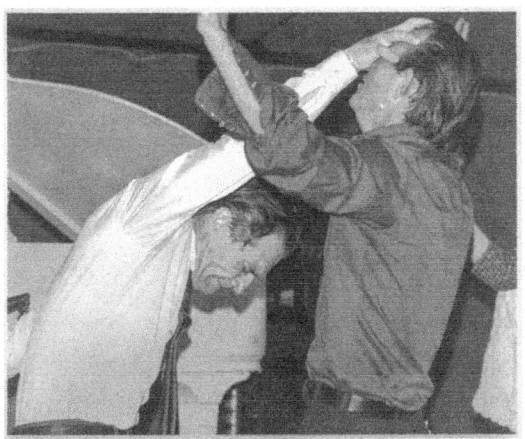

"And Daniel walked into the lion's den and he grabbed the lion by the jaw," he would begin shouting as his congregation chimed in its approval. Finally, climaxing on stories of Christ's miracles, he would transition to his own brand of healing.

He would pace through his congregation and begin pointing at enraptured worshipers. "You have great pain in your knee," he would shout as the woman would answered to his call. Reynolds would grasp the knee with his hands and shout, "Father in the name of Heaven, be thou made whole," he would shout as the woman would jog back and forth in front of the stage.

That was the part of the service I had come to see, those miracles reminiscent of the ones TV preachers would perform on televised revivals. I would jump to my feet and take pictures, forever capturing those moments of rapture.

Naturally, my biggest fear was the Reverend Reynolds would call on me, labeling me as a messenger of the devil. Given my experience setting the Potato Blossom Festival on fire in Presque Isle, Reynolds would have ample evidence to prove his point. Fortunately, he would allow me to take my pictures and go.

I likened myself to an old off key organist, Ray Knight, a projectionist at an adult movie-house. For a small admission fee, one could spend the day watching cinematic classics like *"Screaming Flesh"* with its orgies and perversions. Ray, a silver-haired man with a missing pinky finger, didn't care about the movies. He was interested in playing the old Wurlitzer pipe organ beneath the stage. When the day's screenings were done, he would play until late at night. I identified with Ray and for my TV story he played *"Let Me Call You Sweetheart,"* as he told me of his deal with the devil. He could tolerate the movies as long as he had his organ time. Naturally, my newsroom colleagues didn't see my sincerity. They thought I was only satisfying my own lust. To the contrary, I saw Ray as a kindred spirit, answering a higher call. I had made my devil-deal too, reporting on breaking news while being creative.

I proposed another story about an exotic dancer supporting her family. As I was conducting my interview, the news director from a competing station appeared for the afternoon performance. "What are you doing here?" he asked. "I'm here to interview 'Ebony Princess.' What about you?" He rolled up his magazine and left. With subsequent bosses I had a hard time selling my philosophy. They saw me as something less than a hard-boiled news reporter and constantly tested my sincerity, sending me to car accidents and house fires. Eventually, my bosses came to accept me as a free spirit storyteller. No one could deliver a feature story like I could. I proved it with a Ferrari.

DRIVING THE FERRARI

Rumors were flying that actor Tom Selleck was moving to Falmouth, an upscale seaside town. Naturally, my chances of landing an interview with the *Magnum P.I.* stars were impossible. So, I suggested an alternative story-line. I proposed that locals spotting Selleck had actually seen me, a man of similar appearance. I would dress as the Hawaii sleuth, wearing the flowered shirt, baseball hat and dark glasses and smoking a cigar. To complete the illusion, I borrowed a Ferrari Testa Rossa from a local attorney.

On a Falmouth back road, I met up with the attorney for hasty driving tips. Geared for racing, the Ferrari would stall at the normal speed limit. So keeping the car functioning was difficult enough. Then, because Tom Selleck did not wear glasses, I ditched my own, rendering the road ahead blurry. Frightened and half blind, I was not having fun and decided to bring my project to a close, taking the first exit. From there I would take the back road to the city. I turned the car around on the narrow pavement and heard a thud as the car struck a rock. Perhaps I had struck something on the underside of the car. No one would notice. The attorney noticed, of course, solemnly observing the large chunk of bodywork missing from the front bumper. "I'm sure we'll fix it," I assured him. "I am sure you will," he replied.

Back in the office, my boss buried his head in his hands and sighed. "You know what they do in China," he said. He meant public humiliation, the method Chairman Mao used to punish intellectuals by parading them in the streets. On the office intercom, my boss invited anyone interested to visit our newsroom, there to hear how I had damaged a Ferrari. Not since the company holiday party had I seen so many coworkers, secretaries, salespeople, technicians, even the maintenance man, all clustered in our office. My moment of disgrace became their coffee break. For years, I have borne that guilt. I would drive a parade of my own cars to their rusty graves and never dent one of them. Even Tom Selleck's reverse mortgage commercials brings it all back - my misspent manhood and the desecrated Testa Rossa.

RATS ON THE RUN, WALLABIES ON THE LAM

You didn't have to be a genius to report for television, only a primate with the strength to hold a microphone. Opposing thumbs were optional. Your story could be stellar or mediocre as long as it fit the time format. As a news director once said, "You've got 90 seconds to tell your story or, in the case of Christ's Second Coming, two minutes." Time was the great equalizer. Sometimes my stories were mishmashes of garbled facts. On the other hand, they were so short, one had no time to consider how bad they could be.

Once, the boss sent me to a Maine village gripped by fear. As townspeople told it, rats were turning up everywhere and nerves were on edge. "How does one photograph fear?" I wanted to know. It was hard to tell a rat story unless one could find rats. They operate on their own schedule, usually after dark and always out of sight. My partner and I were striking out. No rats, no story. Then we spotted a dog with a rat in his stomach - it's epitaph, a long, stringy tail hanging from the dog's mouth. We videotaped the dog and headed back to the station, our mission accomplished. That evening, our anchors reported on the rat invasion and their pictures showed the happy pup with a tail in his teeth. The next morning, I got the boss's memo: "Why was it necessary to show a dog with a rat in his teeth? " Why indeed? How else was I to describe the rodent attack on a small Maine town? I had bitten off more than I could chew.

Later, I redeemed myself when I found wallabies on the lam from a wild animal park. The small, kangaroo-like animals had slipped through the fence and taken off into the nearby woods. It was growing dark as I drove up to the York Wild Animal Park in Southern Maine. I was sure the chances would be slim of capturing wallabies on the run. I would be returning empty-handed again, a wallaby wannabe, a reporter unable to bag the big story. My boss would be hopping mad. As I drove up to the park, I saw the glow of tiny eyes in the woods. Clinging together, the wallabies had blown their cover by staring at my headlights. Rounding them up was easy. Furthermore, I had discovered a wallaby hunting technique should I ever choose to roam Australia's Outback. It's amazing, the knowledge one could collect on the truth trail. I could claim my place in the pantheon of great reporters. Journalists had reported from foxholes. I had found the wallabies.

"A WOMAN NEEDS A MAN LIKE A FISH NEEDS A BICYCLE."

Sure I was a late bloomer. It made me the perfect TV journalist, an uninformed celebrity. I could present myself as knowledgeable without knowing much. Everything was news to me. Knowing that limitation, my boss assigned me to stories requiring only patience and a pulse.

One was to ride an elephant in the Ringling Brothers Circus parade through the center of town. It required only one basic skill, spreading my legs as far apart as possible while I rode the elephant through town. It sounds eerily similar to that drugstore "Butt Paste" advice about the rash on my bottom: "Sleep with your legs open." The only difference was the elephant.

On that hot June day, I grasped the rope on the neck of the pachyderm as it sauntered through the city. It was a proud professional moment, demanding little of me. At the parade's end, trainers put water-buckets at the elephants' feet where they sucked it in through their trunks. Then they would spray the water on their backs and, of course, on the riders who sat there. Covered with elephant discharge, I returned to the newsroom to write my story. The day had grown hot and humid, the other reporters in the crowded office gasping for air. "Something stinks in here," growled one. I reminded them that the circus was in town, its animals generating that barnyard smell. In other words, I lay the blame entirely on the animals. The elephants and their sloppy bathing habits were responsible. As in my Presque Isle smoke bomb, I had obfuscated responsibility.

I ignored the elephant in the room. Except in relationships, I never made the same mistake twice. That's why people trusted me, among them a Maine ferry boat captain. He gave me control of a ferry full of cars and commuters as it made its way back from Maine island. With a girlfriend, I had spent the night in a bed and breakfast on North Haven Island off Rockland. Summoning me to the wheelhouse, the captain put my hand on the steering lever and told me I was on my own. Outside, tourists snapped seascape pictures not knowing the maritime peril they faced. They didn't notice that the old state-run ferry was weaving back and forth as I whipped the rudder. A slight turn of the rudder became a sharp shift to the left and right. Like my first driving lesson in Pop's Pontiac, I couldn't keep the ferry on course. The captain wasn't much help. A voice crackled from the overhead radio as another ferry passed. "You boys got a submarine chasin' you?" he laughed. "No," replied my captain. "Well then, how come you're zig-zaggin' 'cross the bay?"

TAKING ON WATER

My maiden voyage in matrimony was equally unstable. For two years, I had the feeling that a submarine was on my tail too, a U-boat with me in the cross-hairs. I married my swimming teacher at the Y.W.C.A., where I treaded water in love's deep end. I was afraid of water until she taught me how to hold my breath and float on my back. That was also how I got along with her. Through our courtship, I learned how to scuba dive and rescue people from drowning. Inspired by Olympic Gold Medal swimmer Mark Spitz, I wore a red, white and blue Speedo, strutting poolside on alert for drowning victims. In truth, I was the one most likely to drown. I still couldn't swim well, advancing through Red Cross training as her pet student. That turned to heavy petting at her house during a Saturday night party. Our lip locking was complicated by one technicality. She was married, her husband kissing another swim teacher in another room. Our sea-monkeying around became habitual, and soon she and I were double dating with the other couple. Out on the town, we made an odd foursome knoodling in the shadows.

Philandering was almost expected of TV reporters but she feared she would be seen by her bosses. It was, after all, the Young

Women's Christian Association, presumably a paragon of high moral values. Instead, we kept our gatherings under wraps. As her husband kissed his girlfriend, I would serenade the couple with flamenco guitar riffs, picking until my figures were numb. I prayed the couple would consummate before my fingers fell off. My swim instructor divorced and by the following winter, Groundhog Day, we were tying the knot in a civil ceremony.

Had Punxsutawney Phil been there, he would have predicted two years of bitter cold. She insisted on keeping her unmarried name. She said it was the feminist thing to do, the first clue that our decisions would be based on what was good for women in general. That would include travel to women's political conventions and man-bashing social activities. I was explained away as "sympathetic press," a journalist presumed to be on their side. That gave me special privileges, including a hotel room to myself while my wife partied with friends down the hall. Her agenda came first - even on the night my TV station aired my first ever documentary. My show about landfills coincided with her political meeting in a small motel. While her colleagues discussed the Equal Rights Amendment, I watched my work on a TV set in the cocktail lounge. For an hour, I watched a video of urban trash bulldozed from one side of the screen to another. To the lounge drinkers around me, it made no sense. By the time they connected the skinny reporter on the screen with me cowering in the corner, the show was over.

My marriage soon mirrored that experience, my good intentions bulldozed into a landfill. Maybe that was the price of love, I thought. It got worse as my role as the man in her life diminished. I was too close, too naive to see it happening. After another of her meetings in Cambridge, Massachusetts, her group moved to a local restaurant, The Thorn and the Rose. In keeping with the feminist theme, it offered no table service and workers, all women, had shaved their heads and wore white robes. They acted uneasy around me, a man in a restaurant for women. My wife later explained that I was allowed to dine there for that one occasion and no more. That was okay by me. I like to believe that I would have complained of hypocrisy, jumping on the table shouting carpe diem! I was too timid and too hungry...

It reminded me of the night I caught my girlfriend making out with a music writer. We had stopped to visit him at his Cambridge home where he regaled us with stories of his Warren Zevon telephone interview. I let the two old friends visit as I snoozed on the couch. When I awoke, they had moved on from Zevon to tonsil hockey. A reasonable man would have jumped to his feet shouting "Werewolves of London!" as he ripped out the man's heart. But cooler heads prevailed and I drove her home. That was my style, the gift of my loving mother.

For the rest of her life, she would watch my failed attempts at love cut short by loveless people. "Some day," she would tell me, "Someone will appreciate what a beautiful person you are." And sometimes, my mothers soft voice was all I heard. During those pandemic days so far in my future, her voice would continue to comfort me. Those nights of lonely lockdown, I could sleep to the sound of her whisper.

MY NAME IS BOND, JAMES BOND.

As a virile young man, I wanted to be James Bond. I would read Ian Flemming's paperbacks, racing from one sex scene to another. Saving the world from madmen was nothing compared to the love Bond would make on a Caribbean beach. One summer, I swooned through the whole series. As an adult, I still longed to have the James Bond suave, able to seduce with a wink and a nod. One of my reporting colleagues had that Bond persona. Michael constantly wore makeup and spoke in syrupy tones. He wore expensive suits to even the most mundane stories because his father told him to "Dress where you want to be." When he got a job in San Diego, he called our Maine newsroom to describe his work environment by the bay. He cooed about dolphins cavorting past his window as he worked. As the saying goes, "He could talk a cat off a fish wagon." He moved on, becoming a media consultant and political operative. But his fast track fame took an ugly turn one day when his wife caught him with another woman. When the police arrived, his wife was burning his tuxedos on their back porch and beating him with a stick.

So much for that Bond wannabe. I clung to the Bond dream, easily adapting to the actors who assumed the role. After Sean

Connery followed Roger Moore, the silken voiced British actor. I was thrilled when he came to Maine in 1990 to film another movie. I longed to cover the story, hoping that some of his charm would rub off on me. Filmmakers had set up shop on the Southern Maine coast that summer, shooting "Bed and Breakfast," a light drama about a man found washed up on the seashore. He had been nursed back to health by a beautiful woman, Talia Shire, the actress best known as girlfriend of boxer Rocky Balboa. Now, an officious film publicist was driving us down the beach trail to the sight of the film work. Shire was walking the seashore in the scene leading up to discovery of the Englishman. My photographer, Jim O'Rourke, and I were ordered to stay in one spot as the actor and director blocked the boring scene. In frustration, O'Rourke and I slipped out of sight and back to a clearing where large recreational vehicles had been parked.

Suddenly, Moore appeared from his RV and sauntered over to the snack table. His face was covered with stage-blood, his shirt torn. He looked every bit the man who would have been disgorged by the ocean. Only the plate of cheese and crackers gave him away. "Mr. Moore," I ventured. "Can I have a word with you?" He graciously accepted and I stumbled through my stock questions about the movie plot and Maine weather. Then, I got to the point, "It's not every man who is rescued by the likes of Talia Shire," I offered. "Yes," he sighed in his signature voice, "She is a lucky woman, isn't she?"

I DID IT MY WAY

Years later, the pandemic would allow me to better understand my fascination with James Bond, the legendary character that melted hearts. In the loneliness of my home, I had time to think about the people who influenced me and how.

When I could have been inspired by Gandhi or Mother Teresa, I chose the mythical Bond, a man who rocketed his Aston Martin through Monte Carlo. There had to be a reason for that obsession - my life in Fantasy Land.

Portland, Maine was the perfect city in which to nurture my fantasies. Its main street, Congress Street, was like the boardwalk to my imaginary amusement park full of clowns and acrobats, some of them elected to public office.

My favorite stop was the record shop where one could find the latest LP's and concert tickets. That was where I first met Shirley, an older blind woman who bought Frank Sinatra records there. Through his music, she could see the world in ways we could not, transported to exotic places through his soft and soulful voice.

Through childhood, she had been comforted by him though she never saw him. His voice was sufficient and through the day and night, she would play his records as she felt the soft ocean breeze through her window.

I empathize with her. Frank Sinatra had serenaded me through my first love affair, a forbidden fling with an older woman in Connecticut. As a welfare mother of four, she was connected to my work as a VISTA Volunteer. On a secret getaway weekend to Cape Cod, we passed the night embrace as Sinatra sang on the radio. "Once in a while, along the way, love's been good to me," he crooned, the Rod McKuen poem about a man whose loves were short but beautiful.

Mine were too, and the song spoke to my love hungry heart. Though our love affair did not last, the song haunts me still. My lover haunted me too. In intimate moments later with other women, I would blurt out "Jean," my first lover's name. Sinatra's music had that effect on me.

I understood the spiritual level at which Shirley, the sightless woman, survived. I shared her passion when Sinatra announced a live concert in our city. At the old downtown record shop, we each bought tickets to the show at the Cumberland County Civic Center..

He opened with reminiscences of Old Orchard Beach, Maine, not far away. It was the place where he first performed with Tommy Dorsey's band. The Pier Casino Ballroom no longer exists but one can still sit on the pier and remember the likes of Sinatra and Duke Ellington performing there. Sinatra recalled the night their bus driver backed over all their instruments. With borrowed instruments from the local high school, the show went on. He finished his concert with his signature "New York, New York," the song to which Times Square lovers kiss on New Year's Eve.

Sightless, Shirley would not have known about the barriers separating her from Sinatra.They were the burly bodyguards who prevented fans from storming the stage. She believed she could walk unrestrained to meet Frank, and no one told her she could not. Guards stopped her and sent her back to her seat.

After the show, Sinatra asked to speak with her. The same bodyguards who had corralled her during the concert were now escorting her backstage. Sinatra was gentle and gracious, saying how much he appreciated her love. Back home, Shirley could add that memory to her beautiful portfolio. Had she not been liberated by her own blindness, Shirley could never have experienced Frank the way she did.

By the same token, without COVID, I would never have relived the stories that became part of my character. Sitting home alone allowed me to breathe air into lifeless memories.

Their senses battered by the internet and social media, the young could not appreciate that story, the old singer of love songs and Shirley, sightless but forever young.

TIPTOE THROUGH THE TULIPS

I had my own favorite singers - among them, Tiny Tim, the quirky long haired man with pale skin and a strained falsetto. I can't say that I would have stormed the stage to be near him, but I did have one unique experience, a visit in his hotel room and a personal serenade. He had been an American icon, singing classic old songs with his ukulele. His hit "Tiptoe Through the Tulips" topped the national charts as America watched his performances. His renditions of early American songs made him a cult hero. His marriage to teen "Miss Vicki" was a national phenomenon, broadcasted live on the Johnny Carson Show.

But Tiny Tim's dominance quickly faded as Americans moved on to other show business characters. In time, Tim divorced "Miss Vicki" and was relegated to shows at country fairs, bare-knuckle nightclubs and finally to a dingy cocktail lounge in Portland, Maine. There he had become a last minute fill-in act. That's how I met Tiny Tim and spent with him those cherished moments. In the lounge earlier, Tim belted old favorites like *"Swanee River"* for those midweek patrons. Maine was often known for entertainers on the downside of their careers. A two hour drive from Boston, it was a popular side stop on the New England tour. Charitably, it was like a bookstore bargain table where they sold remainders of once popular books. That is how the once famous star came to Portland, ignored by the media except for one young man with a taste for irony.

That magical night when Tiny Tim performed at Portland, Maine's Eastland Hotel and then sang a private concert for me in his room.

I didn't have to convince my boss to cover the performance. Nothing else ever happened in the city after dark and none of my colleagues competed to cover the story. It was all mine, Tiny Tim's first and last appearance in a lounge whose headline act had canceled. The city's only other entertainment option that night was professional wrestling at the Expo. He needed no security detail as no one bothered him on his walk down the main street. To passers-by, he was just another odd visitor on a tour of the city. I was the designated reporter for those unconventional people. Most of them at our reception desk had been referred to me, including the old man dressed as Abraham

Lincoln, the fellow with a skunk on his shoulder and the chimpanzee who roller skated down our corridor. I was the go-to man for the misbegotten. It was preordained that I cover Tiny Tim, the almost newsworthy singer.

After the rousing lounge show, he graciously signed autographs for local fans. Management had set his table adjacent to the coat rack, its subtle way of flushing out those who would not have ordered another highball. In the privacy of his room, he mused about the collapse of his marriage while promising there would never be another "Mrs. Tim." He would never remove his wedding ring having resisted sex with another woman for two years and two months... He intimated Miss Vicki, now a New Jersey stripper, had fallen further and faster than he did. No divorcee would want to admit that his mate had moved on to something better. I would joke about my ex-spouse who married a nuclear scientist. "Nuclear physics?" I would joke with her. "How's the fission?" Tim was no different, clinging to that moral high ground when Miss Vicki moved on. Then, just for me, he strummed the ukulele chords to "The University of Maine Fight Song," a drinking tune popular at sporting events and fraternity parties. One could easily imagine a young inebriated fraternity brother guzzling suds before the game.

Now, that boisterous tune had been softened by falsetto as Tiny Tim grinned his over-sized teeth and brushed back his hair. There was nothing like him, my interview lost forever had I not chosen to save it. Now, in the throes of the pandemic, I would watch it on my computer and marvel about those simple times when Tim was noteworthy, if only for a moment.

AND THAT'S THE WAY IT IS.

I got another chance to mingle with greatness when Walter Cronkite came to town. "The most trusted man in America," was an inveterate sailor. He had often sailed Maine's rocky coast, photographing his journey. Cronkite had just published a book on his adventures and had agreed to stop at a local store for a signing.

I was tasked with interviewing him before the store opened, our conversation to be broadcast live on the noon news. I knew of one fundamental mistake of a bad interviewer. Never ask an author what his book is about. It's like asking Beethoven to explain his symphonies. As I waited for Cronkite to arrive, I ran through pertinent questions about sailing. What was it like and how did it compare to anchoring the national news? I had learned about sailing through a college course. They taught me to lower my head when the boat shifted course or risk a beaning by the sail boom. They also taught me that once seasick, I would be praying to die and be fed to the sharks. I hadn't enjoyed sailing, my wife's passion.

She enjoyed sun fishing in the harbor channel. There I was sure we would be run down by an oil tanker, never again to be heard from. I was not competent in the ocean. Once, I had taken my daughter, then ten, for a sail in an inflatable lifeboat. Just feet from the rocks, I felt the current grab us and suck us away from shore. With the oars, I flailed away at the water and couldn't find an effective rowing rhythm. "Daddy?" my daughter asked me. "Are we going to China?" "I don't know, honey," I said, sure that we would be missing at sea. That was the extent of my sailing experience, hardly enough to form a provocative interview. That left the one question I had vowed not to ask. It came out like oil from the Exxon Valdez, the question posed on a million mindless morning shows. "What is your book about?" I asked, as Cronkite glared at me. Already, our interview was taking on water, Cronkite clearly annoyed. He wanted to return the volley by asking "What are you about?"

That was the end of our interview, the longest five minutes of our lives. I don't remember his response. Nor was I asked to join him on the next leg of his journey. I should have known better since I had written a book myself, a collection of feature stories about local people. *Dave's People* chronicled a man who fed pigeons, a weight guesser and a prison inmate who collected fish. A local publisher had bought the manuscript thinking that a book by a local celebrity would sell well. He offered me 15% of the jacket price, $1.50. That meant that for every 100 books they sold, I would earn $150. This was big. That wasn't the point. I had become an author, a small market Walter Cronkite, with all the cache of a literary man. "What is my book about?" I would respond to the local interviewer. "It is about 200 pages." I celebrated the day the bookstore put my product on the shelf. I expected my writing career to take off in the manner of Stephen King. I watched weeks elapse with no news, no request for a second printing. Worse, the store owner moved my book to the $1 bargain table. That made it cheaper than a Presto log and a lot more combustible… One day, a man stopped me in the shopping center parking lot. He said he had seen my book on sale but didn't buy it. I offered him a dollar. "No thanks," he said, and walked away.

Weeks later came death by a thousand paper cuts. The store owner was about to haul my books to a landfill unless I bought them. "What if I don't buy them?" I asked. "They'll go to the dump," he replied. I was about to ask "What dump?" but thought better of it. The idea of fighting off seagulls to salvage my book didn't sound appealing. I hated those birds anyway, remembering my sailing class and their cackling as I emptied my stomach into the ocean. My book deserved a better fate than a garbage dump. I bought those books, now safe in my garage.

D-DAY AT THE MAINE FESTIVAL

As a feature reporter, I was the station's last resort in case of emergency. When a hurricane threatened our coast, I was sent out to find and record damage. The hurricane veered out to sea, leaving me nothing to report. I was about to give up when I saw a delivery truck wipe out the awning of a local hotel. Though not storm related, I explained that fear of the hurricane had made people behave erratically. I never let the facts get in the way of a good story.

On the other hand, a story could break behind me and I wouldn't have noticed. That is what happened the day a dancer tried to recreate D-Day. Instead, she created a disaster. Had she rehearsed it, she could have saved embarrassment while saving Private Ryan. The event was front and center at the Maine Festival, a Bowdoin College exposition of arts, crafts and music. It also featured creative endeavors of invited guests. I was assigned to cover it to promote its weekend activities. The New York City based dancer conceived of a D-Day battle reenactment featuring air raid sirens and farm animals. Dressed in a white jumpsuit, she would meme American air power, swooping in to save humanity. I would cover it live for our evening news, recounting the history as she "flew" over farmland. The air raid sirens were portrayed by women in white robes, wailing from the sidelines. On cue, the women wailed as the dancer entered the animal pen, arms outstretched. She wove through the sheep and goats.

Apparently the animals had not been briefed on her plan. Frightened by the wailing women and unnerved by the dancer, they darted inside the pen and defecated on the grass. In moments, piles of animal leavings had accumulated as the dancer slipped and slid through the manure. She fell frequently, turning her white jumpsuit into a Rorschach test of fecal matter. Mercifully, our live shot ended as the dancer pondered what had gone wrong. Back at the studio, technicians were still guffawing over the live shot and how focused I was on the camera. For the animals, it was bad enough being someone's 4-H project but the "invasion" was more than they deserved. As always, I sided with the animals. Someone once decided that animals were a great source of food and labor, our meals and beasts of burden. We even used them as a source of measurement for combustion engines grading them by the power of horses. Now, against their will, they were used as props in a dance recital. No wonder they were annoyed.

I understood animals, seeing something in their souls. I especially loved llamas, the great creatures of the Andes. I knew them to guard cattle against mountain lions and obediently carry provisions for mountain treks. I also knew they were popular service animals for people with autism and other disorders. Something about the llama helps them be tranquil. That is why I was in love with the two baby llamas of a Eureka couple. They were a surprise, since the mothers hid their pregnancies until the calves popped out. I tried to pose for pictures with the llamas but they were having none of it. There was too much to do and I had a poor track record with animals. I enticed them with grain and sat on the ground, but the llamas ignored me.

They weren't the first. Then, I began singing to them, the great Simon and Garfunkel song "El Condor Pasa." The Peruvian folksong went, "I'd rather be a hammer than a nail..." Slowly, the llamas gathered to listen to my song, their ears focused, their noses sniffing the air. "Not bad," I thought I heard one of them sigh. "Every climb up the mountain begins with a single-step."

SEX FOR SALE

Locked down by the pandemic, I sought human connection with whoever I could find it. My options were limited to supermarkets where I imagined chance encounters in the cat food aisle: "Wow, you have cats too? What a coincidence," I would say. "Say, let's share cat stories over lunch." I was fair game for internet predators, promising love notes for a little spending money. Their photo, if they offered one, was usually of someone else. Through the internet, a woman in Bogota, Colombia promised a rain-forest romance with morning coffee and kisses. She wanted to visit me along with her children, mother and other assorted acquaintances. All I had to do was file the immigration paperwork and give them a place to live. That would be one costly cup of coffee.

Another promised hot tub love with chocolate and champagne. She claimed to be in window frame sales in Cairo, known for its poorly ventilated structures. Just look at the pyramids. All she needed was cash to pay her laborers. She would reimburse me when she returned to the U.S. She grew indignant when I doubted her story, especially when I traced her cellphone number to an Orange County motel. I had good reason to doubt her.. Her internet photo looked like movie star Felicity Huffman in a judicial robe. For the record, Huffman appeared as a judge in the made-for-TV movie *Reversible Errors*. Dealing with these losers was a waste of time, but I had no better use for it. And what if the stories were true? Didn't I deserve unconditional love like that? I had reverted to the teenager perpetually in love with Connie Francis in *Where the Boys Are*, the movie that inspired the first Florida spring break.

I envied the ability of some of my colleagues to find romance while I could not. Their success was puzzling. I hoped that my vocation as a broadcaster would make me desirable, a theory based on my amorous coworkers. Our TV weatherman would spend evenings at local cocktail lounges passing out phone numbers. Spotting a likely love candidate, he would send a cocktail with his business card. Sometimes it would bear his pick-up line: "Let's prestidigitate on the dance floor and trip the light fantastic." That meant he wanted to dance. In the language of his profession: Art was an advancing warm front with the likelihood of property damage. He admitted that his flirtation rarely worked, one chance in a thousand. But there was always that chance, he said. Another colleague, Tracy, a news photographer, pursued women based on their market value. He lived rent-free in his girlfriend's house. She lived with her parents because they did not want her on her own until she was older. She was 25 and much too naive for the real world, they thought... I often visited with him there on my lunch break. I loved his wild side, once claiming to bed three women in the same day by plying them with pot.

On long and tedious assignments, he would regale me with stories, two infantrymen hunkered down against the enemy. One night, we were sent to a protest, activists vowing to stop construction of a nuclear power plant. Under a full-moon, we marched across a salt marsh to the construction site of the Seabrook, New Hampshire plant. The protesters' plan was to storm the site, banish the workers and create a vegetable garden. We joined them as they approached the cyclone fencing, state police and guard dogs poised to defend the property. Things fizzled, of course. No one wanted to tangle with an angry German Shepard. Besides, no one had brought vegetables for the garden. Furthermore, the tide had risen and our muddy path to the plant was now submerged in seawater. We had two options, wait for the low-tide six hours away or forge the tidal rivers back to our cars. That was our choice, our camera gear held over our heads as water lapped at my belt-buckle.

Today, one can see the marsh through which we marched. It is in the foreground of that plant, now 30 years old. It claims to provide safe and reliable energy to New England. I will also remember it as the plant that fueled my beautiful memories of the moon, the marsh and the soothing sea water saturating my pants.

INTERVIEW WITH A NAZI

Once, at a police convention we were covering, my photographer friend bought an old service revolver, storing it in his girlfriend's antique dresser. We often combined business with pleasure, visiting him at the home of his girlfriend. Weeks later on a visit, he pulled the gun from the dresser drawer and waved it around. He cocked the hammer and pulled the trigger. It discharged, the bullet ricocheting off the ceiling and rolling across the floor. It begged the question why the gun was loaded to begin with. But with my friend, it was best not to ask and the mystery was part of his charm. Conversely, he was charmed by my innocence.

One night, we used his house to interview a Maine Nazi. Using the name Karl Vogel, the man purported to lead a New England white supremacy group. For the interview, he wore military regalia and hung their swastika on the wall behind him. As a condition for the TV interview, we "backlit" him, flooding the wall with light but casting him as a shadow. For the series, we also interviewed local civil rights leaders and a rabbi. Evil is its own worst enemy, and the Nazi was exposed in an unintended way. When the film was aired, a technician boosted the video grain, making the man's face bright and clear. The world could see who he was. He called to protest saying I had promised secrecy. "I just saw my face on TV," he yelled. "What kind of TV do you have?" I asked. When he said it was a Sylvania, I had my answer. "I knew it," I said. "That's typical of that brand and not many people own them." Satisfied with my explanation, he hung up. Sometimes I surprised myself.

Still, I was much more comfortable in my innocence, a small town boy watching my cats chase dust bunnies through my apartment. They appreciated that sanctuary and remained prepared to defend it against all enemies, foreign or domestic. That included the girlfriends I would bring home hoping for romance. Once, I convinced a TV station intern, a stunning blonde, to nestle on my couch as we watched PBS. All was going well as I draped my arm over her shoulder. That's when I saw my cats' eyes glowing in the darkness of my kitchen. Trouble was stirring. Both cats broke into a full gallop, their paws thundering on the wooden floor. I had no time to warn my date. In a second, they were scratching up her bare leg on the way to her heaving chest. Her scream startled them and they retreated as they came, digging in to break their descent. So ended our relationship.

Through the years, cats had always been my soulmates. They would comfort me when I was sad and protect me when I felt threatened. As a child, I learned that connection from my first cat. Sparky, a gold and white long-haired kitten, had contracted distemper, giving him a 50-50 chance to survive. The vet advised that love could make a difference. So I kept him in my bed, petting him through the night until his fever broke. It was the first time I had ever saved a life and it made a lasting impression. In my house, cats were for keeps, and no one could interrupt that energy flow.

PRESIDENTIAL FRIENDS

In Maine, broadcast journalism opened doors for me, though I was not always sure what to do with the opportunity. I met celebrities who called Maine home, among them, Gary Merrill, one time husband of Betty Davis. Merrill was known to wear a skirt on hot summer days. He also liked encouraging anti-war protesters who often occupied federal office buildings. Once, they occupied the office of Maine Senator William Cohen while others gathered on the plaza below. As reporters, we hunkered down in the hallway outside the Senator's office during the occupation. Their plan was to stay until the U.S. pulled troops out of Central America. One of the office occupiers passed me a note to drop out the window. Addressed to his wife, it said, "Honey, I won't be home for dinner." Merrill was excited that the protest would be broadcast live on our late-night news and set out to encourage the activists. Following our 11 o'clock live shot, the activists disbursed. It was late and dinner at home was getting cold. I was standing in the dark when Merrill, panting, approached me. "Do you know how hard it is to buy a television set in this town after 11 o'clock?" he groused. Great point. There seemed no end to things to protest.

By the time a native son was elected President, protesting had become unfashionable. When George Herbert Walker Bush was elected U.S. President, he still summered in Maine but rarely encountered protesters. Through his visits, he came to like me through my human interest stories... That's because of my affinity for common folks. Among them was Sanford barber Emile Roy, a charming French Canadien. As the town's only registered Republican, Emile became a GOP folk hero and Bush friend. In fact, the President insisted that Roy visit him at his Kennebunkport compound. There they would visit as Emile trimmed the President's hair and eyebrows.

My story about their friendship made national news and earned me unique prominence. I, too, was often invited to presidential events in Maine as well as Washington D.C. In fact, dropping Emile's name on an elevator in Guangzhou, China got me a Presidential phone call. My wife and I had been staying at the city's White Swan Hotel, the same location where the President was staying on a diplomatic visit. I mentioned Emile to Secret Service agents on that elevator and in moments, Bush called my hotel room. Such was the gravity of my friendship with small town folks. It meant that I got access to the President as no one else in the Maine press could. I proved it through invitations to White House events.

With my daughter Susannah visiting with then-Vice-president George Bush at Walker's Point, the Bush family vacation-home in Kennebunkport, Maine

One cynical colleague said I had sold out to "The Man," but I took such comments in stride. Given the choice, I would eat off White House tableware any time. In fact, I soon got that chance, along with a priceless souvenir. I was invited to a White House luncheon in which the President would dine with local reporters, a goodwill visit with small market scribes like me. I assumed it would be a chummy visit in the Rose Garden, a wine and cheese soiree. Instead, it was a gaggle of small city anchors, the Kens and Barbies of middle America. It had the feel of an Amway convention. In the State Dining room, I toyed with my vegetables as Abraham Lincoln eyed me from his portrait on the wall.

Paraphrasing Lincoln, America would little note, nor long remember me. I had but one mission, as I saw it, get a video of me asking a question - any question. That was the test of a true White House reporter. Even "Why are we here?" would do. A reporter friend always opened a new conference with that question. It made him a running joke among my colleagues. His presence always raised the existential question, "Why is he here?" It must have occurred to his birth parents. I was seated next to John Sununu, Bush's Chief of Staff. He was a dour and portly man who surely posed the same question about me. The conservative former Governor of New Hampshire gave off a threatening vibe, much like the flaring neck of an angry Komodo Dragon. I wondered if it was appropriate to ask for another seat. Instead, I buried my face in the sauteed asparagus.

Bush politely answered questions for others as my hand shot in the air. This was new for me, wanting to be called on. In high school and college, I had avoided attention, praying that the teacher would never call on me. My classroom responses never went well. When my French teacher asked me the meaning of a word, I answered, "Well, this is probably wrong but..." My teacher responded, "You are right. You are wrong." As the class laughed, I decided that I would never again speak in class. Now, so many years later, I was breaking that vow of silence.

My question would address Maine lobster-men and their complaint that Bush's speedboat was interfering with their harvest. The burning Kennebunkport question was, "What was he going to do about it?" It was either that or have him discuss his latest haircut. On TV, the answer didn't matter as much as my on camera question. I never got to ask my question. He didn't call on me and I sat there in stunned silence, my chance at "the big show" was over. I would leave empty-handed, no scoop and no leftovers. Maybe that was why I was attracted to the table napkin at his plate. It would be the only proof I had that I had been close to greatness. I stuffed it in my pocket and slipped past the Secret Service. In my pocket was a napkin stained with cherry cobbler, my honor stained by petty theft.

DEALING WITH THE DEVIL

I needed moral clarity and I got it from an unlikely source, a self-proclaimed Messiah. He would teach me that words matter, and there is danger in broadly labeling people. It is especially true in defining one's faith. Dennis Friel, a biker and sometime felon considered himself a holy man. He loved challenging the boundaries of law and religion. He also reveled in notoriety and hoped to make a living through libel suits. When a number of Maine churches were vandalized, he made public his approval. The churches had been spray-painted with the numbers 666, a biblical reference to evil and the mark of the beast. Friel asserted that churches themselves were evil and the graffiti, a fitting sign. "Those churches were homes of the devil," he said. Naturally, Friel denied responsibility for desecration but publicly supported it. Through numerous press conferences, Friel asserted he was a Christ figure empowered to destroy religious corruption.

All this was over my head. I never covered the story nor was I interested in his thoughts. Still, this was TV news, a national story. As the reporter on duty, I was assigned to write some words about Friel to be read by our anchor. I could have consulted other writers. I didn't do that. It was almost quitting time and I had a tennis lesson. I wrote a short news story based on what little I remembered. ABC network had already labeled him a "Satanist" because of his alleged vandalism. Who else but a "Beast" would motorcycle through Maine spray painting churches?

I was wrong, Friel identified himself as a "Super-Christ," defender of the true "faith." According to him, I had ruined his reputation, grounds for a libel suit. He filed it against me and my company. For a year, I prayed that he would drop his suit. Worse yet, our company attorney played at the same tennis club. I had no place to hide. As the trial date approached, I had visions of my photo splashed on the front page of the paper. "Local Celeb Is Star Witness in Satan Trial," the banner would read. But, I was lucky, fate gave me a pass. When the trial began, the newspaper's court reporter was on vacation. Friel represented himself in the trial and jurors smiled at me as I took the stand. I admitted my mistake but had not intended malice. It seemed plausible. The devil made me do it. Friel lost his case. Years later, I would instruct my journalism students that words matter. I would tell them of a young writer who learned that lesson the hard way. They never asked the identity of the writer and I never told them.

GOING TO THE DOGS

I had one more chance in the court of public opinion, the case of a dog rescuer charged with being a public nuisance. Homeless David Koplow would Shepard his six dogs through city streets, calling them by name. "Here Precious," he would cry out, bringing the wanderers back to the fold. Legends surrounded the reclusive, unshaven man. Some said he had lost his mind in rabbinical school. Still, no one spoke to him as city citations piled up against him. He moved to a smaller city, Biddeford, where he continued his wandering, feeding his dogs fresh fish while he ate food handouts. Authorities cited him there too, and eventually, he had a day in court.

It was packed that day the judge graveled the courtroom to order. City prosecutors alleged that he was flouting the law and mistreating animals. When they finished, Judge Arthur Brennan told Koplow he had a right to defense. "I do?" gasped an incredulous Koplow. He looked around the room to recruit a character witness. Spotting me, he walked over whispering, "Can I call you as a witness?" "I don't think that is a good idea," I replied. I could see the headline: "Local Celeb in Satan Trial Now Defends Dogman."

The case continued, court adjourned, dozens of people lingered in the hallway. The robed judge appeared, working his way through the crowd. He stopped for a moment and looked at me, "You chickenshit," he said smiling and walked away.

COMING TO EUREKA

Leaving my Maine legacy in the dust, I headed West, everything I owned stuffed into a U-Haul trailer hitched to a rusty Subaru. I had hoped someone would beg me to stay - my daughter, ex-wife, old girlfriend - anybody. Not even those wily wallabies would miss me.

I drove west on Interstate 80, the endless artery through the heartland. I had taken a job in Eureka, California, a small TV station in the tiniest market in the country. Only tin cans and string would have been smaller.

But it was TV, dammit, the toxic vocation that ran through my veins. It turned children into TV stars and fender benders into lead stories. Every one of those stories ended with the caveat "It could have been worse."

In house fires, no one was hurt. In accidents, no one was injured. And in bank robberies, the gunman escaped with an "undisclosed amount of cash but no shots were fired." As journalists, we prepared for the likelihood that something big might happen - but never did.

For the young reporters who longed for live shots, it was a disappointment. One couldn't even count on live reports from the Humboldt County Fair, where a man was shot out of a cannon.

That was the big attraction one year and KIEM TV dispatched its star reporter to capture the moment. She stationed herself near the net where the acrobat would land. He would speak with her after the shot. Beforehand, she discussed angle, velocity and descent.

On cue, the man slid into the barrel and, when the cannon discharged, rocketed into the net. Shaken, he staggered off camera and into the crowd.

The reporter stalled for time, reviewing the physics of a flight gone wrong. Mercifully, the live shot ended and the man recovered. It was, after all, Humboldt County where nothing went according to plan. As someone always said, "It could have been worse."

We weren't looking for trouble, but we wanted to be there when it happened. At Pelican Bay State Prison, that was a guarantee. It housed California's most violent criminals with endless ways to make more trouble.

Once I went on a media tour of the prison. With me was a crusty cowboy deejay, Bill Stamps, owner of KPOD in Crescent City. We were crossing the exercise yard at noon when an inmate fight broke out. As they punched and wrestled, corrections officers pepper-sprayed and tear gassed them as guards shot rubber - bullets. Our guide ordered us to stand against the wall. Stamps muttered, "What a bunch of bullshit."

I would later learn that lunchtime fights were common, the one chance inmates had to roundhouse each other. It always happened at the end of the lunch hour so as not to disrupt their meal. To them, a riot was worth time in the cooler.

Their only other diversions were self-tattooing and watching local TV, the only available channel. They would send notes and drawings to our female reporters. As accomplished artists, they would draw attractive young women posing next to "lowriders", older model cars, streamlined, lowered and covered with chrome ornaments. Presumably, the pictures represented the life inmates hoped to lead on their release.

Reporters were both flattered and frightened by those letters, fearful that once released, inmates would kidnap them and take them to live in Fresno. I saw no difference between inmates and the local barfly's already chasing them.

I loved the idea that convicts would watch me on the news and soon I was writing back. I didn't mind being a "kite," which is prison lingo for one who forwards letters to someone else. I was honored to be an extension of the US. Postal Service.

That finally led to my visits with inmates living in the Security Housing Unit in Pelican Bay (SHU). That is where they housed "the worst of the worst," and visiting them gave me a sense of purpose.

I was also intrigued by the women who married them, busing all the way from Southern California to visit them.

INSIDE THE DUNGEON

Just like my winter lock-down, inmates in the SHU rarely saw daylight, except when visitors came. That is when they were permitted visits through glass, conversing by telephone. As we spoke, he could look over my shoulder and see the sun. My friend was an amiable, young, San Diego Latino, conversing entirely in Spanish. This was my way of practicing the language. I soon learned the words for: judge, jury and wrongful conviction. He was a San Diego gang leader, enforcing dominance with a gun. He was convicted for two murders, although there were surely more. He was also known as an escape risk after he promised to blow out the concrete walls of his cell.

One day, prison officials told me that I could visit my friend in an open room, his first chance in years to do so. He seemed nervous walking into a room filled with families and loving couples. He took his seat in the corner. There, no one could approach him from behind. His eyes darted around the room as he spoke. Suddenly, another inmate approached him bearing two vending machine burritos. Before my friend could take them, a corrections officer grabbed them. "No inmate-to-inmate gifts," he barked, tossing them into the trash. "I could have eaten them," I whined, having missed my breakfast.

Moments later, my friend stopped talking and said he would have to return to the cell. Something had clearly spooked him, though it took months to figure out what. The burritos were likely a goodwill offering to him because of his gang leadership and prison yard clout. With a nod, he could still order a hit on anyone. The burritos were the Pelican Bay equivalents to gold, frankincense and myrrh, gifts to a gangland deity.

HOW PRISON PREPARED ME FOR THE PANDEMIC

My pandemic year on lock-down helped me empathize with inmates, isolated from day-to-day discourse. My incarcerated brother told me that outside, we make 300 decisions a day - what to eat, when to sleep and what to do. He was limited to just 30, all under someone's watchful eye.

I understood what he was talking about. We would fight over a gas pump or a parking space, venting out anger on the innocent. Even homeless people fought about sleeping spots. In a city full of vacant stores, two fought for space in the entry of a shoe store. It led to busting out its front window with a hammer. They didn't take any merchandise because that was not the point. Everyone watched each other. To violate mask-wearing was to risk the devil's wrath. It reminded me of those school snitches who would bust you for running in the hallway. I was one of them, a 5th grade crossing guard. With my stop sign and chrome whistle, I would inform on classmates who ran in the crosswalk. The teacher would say, "It has come to my attention there have been shenanigans crossing the street." My classmates would look at me, the whistle-blower, the informant. I deserved a new identity and police protection.

In the pandemic, I reverted to my childhood. I would be working from home, relying on old friendships without the opportunity to find new ones. How I ate, where I shopped, with whom I associated, all became subject to COVID restrictions. They included social distancing and limited access to loving people. There was no hugging, hand-shaking, kissing or caressing. It reminded me of those inmates shut off from the same. And it explained how an inmate friend of mine and his fiance got in trouble with a single, loving touch. The two would coo the day away in the visitors' area, mindful of prison restrictions about social contact. Several hours into the visit, they made a bold move, a loving touch in a private place. They thought that near the microwave oven, they would not be caught on the surveillance camera. So the woman, Lisa, swiped her hand against Sonny's crotch ever so gently. How gently and where? It didn't matter to the corrections officers who pounced on the couple sending Lisa on her way and Sonny back to solitary. She was barred from visits for the next six months.

With that same sense of separation, I faced life on lock-down along with everyone else. And like inmates, we paid the price of isolation. I would watch infomercials selling knives and collectible coins. I spent several thousand dollars buying things on eBay, thrilled when the package arrived. They included bagpipes, two saxophones, an oboe, a trumpet, two guitars and five clarinets. I also bought a Mortimer Snerd ventriloquist dummy, a roulette wheel and a Vietnamese telephone. I had everything I needed to survive the social meltdown should it happen. I even bought a Presidential Medal of Freedom to award myself. It would be a proud American moment, bestowed during my "State of the Cats Address."

THE CAR KEY AND THE STOVE BOLT

As News Director in Eureka, I could have used gangland clout. My reporters were wannabe toughies, at least one of whom needed a long walk down the railroad track with mobster Bugsy Siegel. It is the only language he understood. My boss was a primadonna who would have threatened me with cement loafers if she thought she could. I tried hard to please her but often got the message from her lieutenant, the Chief Engineer. He would tell me, "The boss ain't pleased. She ain't pleased at all." The message chilled me. The boss would complain about workers being late. "Fix it," she would snarl. I would do so the corporate way, and put a letter of reprimand in her personnel file. Then the boss would haul me into her tiny office to "rip me a new one," as the kids would say. "What the hell did you do that for?" demanded the boss. I knew there was no viable answer, only a 45 slug from my attorneys Smith and Wesson. I would have preferred waking up next to a dead horse.

Then there was the car key caper. Reporters were always losing them after draining the tank of gasoline. The result was a rolling news fleet that wouldn't make it out of the parking lot. We were the laughing stock of the livestock next door. This required keen leadership on my part. I reached back into family history to develop my idea. I remembered the L.A. gas station where the mechanic recommended hot peppers in our radiator. As my brother talked with him, I slipped off to the restroom using the key attached to a block of wood. That was their way of protecting their investment. I bought a large stove bolt and attached the news car ignition key to it. That way, we would always know where the key was, at least with the male drivers. We stopped losing the key, but the men complained that the key and bolt made an unintended bulge in their pants. In mixed company, they were standouts. Once again, I was warned that "The boss ain't pleased." I had to stop the practice. I knew then that my days were numbered.

"I don't think we're going to get along," she told me one day as she cut a third of my pay. I am sure she hoped I would resign in a huff. To her surprise, I didn't. I enrolled in graduate school as an English major. It was, however, annoying. More than anything, that made college worthwhile. Finishing my shift in Eureka, I would pack up to leave for the day. "Where are you going?" she would ask me. "I have an appointment with Hamlet," I would reply. "To be, or not to be?" became the anthem of my new life.

At my next TV job, I worked for a TV boss with a similar demeanor. His leadership mantra: "Lead. Follow. Or, get the hell out of the way." I preferred the third choice. He may not have liked me either, but he liked that Nina had money. He was dumbstruck when she drove up in her silver Lincoln one day to drop off my lunch. "The care home business must be doing well," he marveled. True enough, but to make money you had to clean bedpans. He wasn't ready for that. Once, after cautioning me that "You didn't do what I asked you to do," he threatened me with dismissal. "I could fire you," he said.

"Or I could quit," I replied using Nina's advice. The subject of my termination never came up again. Still, his radiator could boil over at any time.

The boss had entered our news car as a float in the local Rhododendron Parade, a Spring celebration of the local flower. Between school bands and Shriners in those little clown cars, floats would cruise through the city streets as their riders tossed candy to the kids. To be a legitimate float, one had to display bouquets of the flower. Borrowing a car from a local dealership, I yanked rhododendron blossoms from my neighbor's tree and stuck them on the car. All was set but for one detail. I couldn't find the magnetic sign that was to have born our station's call letters. I didn't worry about it. The Macy's Parade would be one thing, Eureka's tiny parade, another. I was enthralled by the grandeur of the moment, my stellar news team waving to the adoring crowd as we inched toward the first reviewing stand. It was a spot on Eureka's landmark Eureka Inn, and the spot from which the local public TV station would broadcast events. I had always wondered about the viewership of that program since most folks could see the festivities in person. At the apogee of the moment, I waved to the adoring crowd and imagined public TV announcers broadcasting my name. Suddenly, the boss's sales manager emerged from the crowd and was yelling at me. "Where's the sign?" he screamed as parade-goers watched in awe. "I don't know," I replied. But the sales manager was livid, his face turning crimson. "The boss is pissed!" he screamed as I considered my options.

One would be to walk away and catch the next Greyhound to San Francisco. I could hear Journey's Steve Perry singing "Don't Stop Believin'." I chose the courageous way. I finished the parade with my news team, went home and sulked. Nothing hardened the spirit like a good pout. In that case, my revenge was my Master's Degree in Teaching of Writing. But then, I could file away my grievances for future reference. Only Strontium-90 has a longer half-life than my grievance file.

LIVING THE FANTASY

Love is often based on the same kind of reverence. We assume that the other lover will validate us and, in the perfect world, insulate us from pain. The pandemic would heighten my need for that security, leading me to meaningless relationships. Should I develop the virus, I would need someone to take me to the hospital and care for me. I wasn't the only one to feel that way. So did shut-ins, people I knew who would call me for the sound of my voice. I had already been down that road, victim to the fantasy that a Caribbean woman could fill my needs - once she had her green card.

My cats have similar fantasies, that those bugs they chased through my house will amount to something. They never do. And yet, my cats continued to chase the dream until they collapsed.

For years after moving to Eureka, I would still get lost in its neighborhoods. Why were there four Cedar Streets, Why did "S" Street suddenly turn into West Street? And how did you pronounce Buhne Street, where we lived? Was it "Booner" or "Boon?" On that street, Nina had died in the crosswalk in front of our home.

Reacting to that grief, I sought replacement love, courting a Caribbean woman by the internet website "Dominican Cupid." In six months, we were legally married and I was arranging for her permanent residence in the U.S. We were 30 years apart in age, but I thought that goodwill and love could conquer all. By the same logic, my cats could live by eating flies. I was so wrong. I hadn't learned a thing from that childhood song: "I don't know why I swallowed the fly. Perhaps I'll die."

With a wife not working, a teenage daughter in private school and many debts, I was headed for trouble. I had swallowed the fly, larvae and all. As the pandemic was sneaking up on the United States, I was futilely trying to save the marriage while dealing with the rash in my shorts. It all imploded on that January Sunday morning when I called the police and my spouse went to jail.

THE UNRAVELING

Handcuffed and barefooted, she walked to the squad car, a uniformed deputy on one side and Spanish translator on the other. Yahindi looked at me with a half-smile as she walked past. How many times had I reported on the "perp walk," a handcuffed somebody shuffling to a squad car. They had been shoplifters and alleged killers - but never a spouse. I knew many who deserved a walk like that - but not Yahindi and not as her daughter watched. I also didn't deserve the abuse that led to her arrest.

We had kissed in the warmth of a Caribbean night and danced to a gentle Latin rhythm. We had ridden a camel on the outskirts of Jerusalem and climbed a Bethlehem hill on Christmas Eve to see the birthplace of Jesus. In those six years, we had lived the fairy tale union of two beautiful souls.

Early that morning, I had shaken myself from sleep. I had promised a local Evangelical Church, Ebenezer Restoration Church, to help them serve the homeless. The sun rose over the hamburger restaurant where church members gathered with clothing, they also had Egg McMuffins and coffee. Pastor Ruben Rodriguez arranged for the gathering, reading first from the NIV Bible scripture:

*Is it not to share your food with the hungry and to provide
the poor wanderer with
shelter - when you see the naked, to clothe them,
and not to turn away from your own flesh and blood?
Then your light will break forth like the dawn...*
Isaiah 58:7-8

Among them was a young woman, Betty, whose husband had abused her. Now she was single and studying to be a nurse. Church members moved to Old Town, Eureka's center and continued to distribute socks, snacks and coffee. Afterwards, I returned to my house where my wife remained in bed surrounded by piles of clothes. I told her about my morning and then offered to buy breakfast. She didn't take the offer well. She lunged at me and grabbed my pants. That's when I called the police. Ten minutes later, she was sitting in a squad car, her daughter tearfully listening as police tried to explain California domestic violence law.

How could I explain to Leticia what I barely understood? I came to understand domestic battery from a new perspective: "I overreacted," people would say. "I brought it on, destroying my family by calling the police." I also saw it from my stepdaughter's point of view. She had just lost her mother in the most shameful way. How could her father have done "that?" I covered a Maine case in which the father fatally stabbed his wife. Yet at his arraignment, their children rushed forward to hug him. Children seek love instinctively. In this case, I had taken it from her.

Our pastor/friend, there at the time of arrest, was not helpful. Like many inexperienced clergy, he said the answer lay in the scripture. That was like telling me to consult my owner's manual after I had crashed the car. Nobody told me before the crash how to use the brake. "How are you going to bail her out?" asked the pastor. "I'm not. I'm going out to be joyful," I said to awkward silence. He hugged Leticia before he left. As a minor league Dr. Phil, he wasn't doing well. He had already asked me when we had last gone on a date. Earlier that week. When had I last brought her flowers? The day before when had I offered to bring home food? Just before she assaulted me. I had followed every directive in those frothy love manuals.

Now it was time to find joy on my own terms. I drove to the makeup company at the shopping mall. There I would hatch my plan to give makeup to ladies at a women's shelter. My late wife Nina always said, "If you want water, you have to dig your own well." I knew what she meant.

FAST TRACK TO JOY

My mother would be proud of her child who crawled at her feet. When I could, I spoke the words forever burnished in my book of baby memories. Alongside my lock of hair, my mother had written: "Baby's first words: "Isn't that nice?" For all the things a child could complain about, runny food, soiled underwear and people talking down to him, I passed off infancy as "nice." I have continued to see "nice" where others wouldn't. Through my 70 plus years, I have seen niceness everywhere. Doing so gives me power over that which I cannot change. Soiled diapers were not "nice," but it sure beat constipation. Being punched in the stomach for selling newspapers at school was not nice. But I have a great writing career to show for it. Divorce is not nice, but it does teach one to travel light.

Naturally, niceness can trouble others if you don't share their misery. My younger brother had that gift for misery. Why else would he have bought a house in the heart of Oakland's most crime infested neighborhood. Police helicopters overhead and frequent gunfire didn't help the curb appeal of the family home. Ultimately, he found ways to share that misery. It happened when our mother, a joyful healer, passed away.

OTHERING

Sowing misery takes patience. It involves marginalizing joyful people like me. They have a name for it now, "othering." It was easier in our sheltered home environment where we, as children, learned to create our own reality. Mine was an imaginative childhood in which I was Hopalong Cassidy, Roy Rogers and Zorro. It made sense that I avoided family outings as too real. I preferred staying at home, free to gambol through my happy world.

My younger brother seemed intent on bursting my protective shield. Once, he discovered that I was horrified by a caterpillar photo in a nature book. Something about the two green creatures with bulging eyes frightened me. The color photo seemed to depict smiley creatures crawling to devour me. It reminded me of the1932 black-and-white horror movie *"Freak Show."* In the Tod Browning film, real circus side-show performers overpower an evil man by trapping him beneath a wagon. The last haunting scene of the movie shows sideshow people crawling toward him through pools of mud. Over time, my younger brother would use that tactic more often. When our mother died, he found a new way to horrify me, stealing her remains from the cemetery. The remains of a saint were spirited away on the luggage-rack of a motorcycle.

Born of missionary parents in the Cape Verde Islands off Africa, she loved her sons, husband and students. She shared that love with me. When she took a job as a tutor in the British West Indies, I flew to visit her. Then, she insisted I take a side trip to Haiti, an hour's flight away. She wanted me to be sure I saw life's full spectrum. Her other sons did not take her mission seriously. My brother Peter used his Mexico trips to smuggle drugs. That would land him in prison.

PETER'S STORY

He had been living with our mother in Visalia and dating her best friend, another teacher. One night when he was not there, police came to search her home. They poured through his book's and tools. They found enough to convict him of many things including drug manufacture and possession of firearms by a felon. The charge was homicide, the murder of a police informant. Court documents said he was a paid assassin - a charge he has not denied.

She had often visited him there, the last time at Folsom Prison outside Sacramento. She and my father were divorced by then, but they rode together to the prison, a solemn last family junket. My impetuous younger brother was not there. I lost a soulmate when my mother died in a Salinas hospital, Nina was with me during my final visit. I helped to arrange her funeral at the Visalia First Baptist Church. A bright young man, a missionary to Russia, described how my mother had inspired him, a beautiful eulogy. For this, my younger brother was present, lying on one of the church pews. She was buried in Moss Landing Cemetery next to her sisters, Virginia and Eunice - a fitting repose.

Months later, though, my younger brother decided that we had buried her contrary to her wishes. When he had the chance - the opening of the grave-site, he grabbed her urn and drove off on his motorcycle. In death, she was taking the ride of her life. For months, we fought over his right to do that without telling us. It led to a lawsuit brought by my older brother, Peter and ended in ugliness. A judge ordered my mother's urn returned.

My father joined my younger brother in the unsuccessful suit. For years I idolized Peter, defending him at every turn. There was no way a man so gentle with me could hurt anyone else. In his final months, I came to realize there was truth in the case against him. Why else would he have made weapons of assassination and associated with people who believed human life was expendable? Why would he have manufactured meth in our mother's house, knowing the danger of its ingredients? And how could my younger brother allow that to happen? I will never know.

I remember a Christmas night when my brothers took me to a Visalia park, there in the darkness, they offered me pills and cocaine. I declined. It is no surprise that I settled in Maine for 20 years, as far as I could get from the vortex. I came to realize that it was the only way I could become the person I wanted to be. I couldn't do it on my own, but being close to them would not have helped. I had to accept that there was something in Peter's psyche that led him to his dark existence. It was frightening to be around. And now in his final months, I could learn to love him as imperfect - but love him just the same.

BROTHERLY CORRESPONDENCE

I had always envied my younger brother and his free spirit hippie lifestyle. It didn't bother me that he converted the basement of our family home to a den for his high school friends.There, they would zone out on acid rock and smoke pot. It made them insatiably giddy and when I would visit, they enjoyed their euphoria. They would speak in coded language, amused that I could not understand them.

I didn't like being an outsider and tried to understand their culture. Alone, I would go to concerts of famous rock performers to watch the shows and the people who attended them.That is what led me to a strange and close encounter with Jim Morrison of The Doors. They were performing at the Earl Warren Showgrounds in Santa Barbara, a large covered arena usually used for boat shows and rodeos. For rock shows, they would project colorful images of cartoons, amoeba and human cells. Presumably, staring at those pictures while The Doors performed would heighten one's senses. It gave me a headache. Additionally, with my necktie and sports coat, I had clearly overdressed for the occasion. I watched The Doors perform "Light My Fire" while nubile young women danced provocatively around me. Naturally, I hoped they would be seduced by my English Leather cologne.

After the concert, I lingered in the snack-bar closing down for the night. A young sweat soaked man in a leather jacket approached the snack bar asking for a Coke. It was Jim Morrison. "Sorry," barked the man at the counter, "We're closed." Morrison looked at me for a moment, and then turned back to the stage. Given the chance, I am sure I would have asked my signature question: "What is 'Light My Fire" about?

My younger brother would have loved that story if he had given me the chance to tell it. He enjoyed observing life as I did, but he wasn't comfortable outside his element. All his friends were quirky and counter-cultural, like photographer Bobby Castro of San Francisco. They were friends when my younger brother lived there, frequently the city's punk community. Castro photographed people, his black and white images capturing punk just as Emily Dickinson wrote of spiders and flies. His obsession made him legendary. Bobby Castro was agoraphobic. Living in his parents' basement, he never left the city, not even to cross the Golden Gate Bridge. Only with his death at 63 did people acknowledge this strange and sheltered behavior. In some ways, my younger brother was like Castro. He never broke character from the aimless and angry motorcyclist. It made sense that he would join his mother in the afterlife, two souls unable to sleep…

He withdrew even more after our father died. At the funeral, he lay on the church pew and in the car on the way to the cemetery. He said he was afraid "they" were out to get him. He chose my father's gravesite to break off our relationship for good. He said, "This is the last time I will be speaking to you." He kept his promise. I have not heard the sound of his voice since that day. Over the years, I would send emails, hoping he had changed his mind. I have kept them all, along with his biting responses... When he told me not to come to his son's wedding, he wrote, "My stomach really does turn over when I picture you schmoozing it up (or, at least attempting to) with my son Calder." At the wedding, he did not speak to me. When I suggested that we repair our relationship in the afterlife, he responded, "So now you believe in reincarnation enough to suggest that I would have to know you again in another life?????? You wanna add insane to my list of your attributes???" So, there we had it, two dis-associative brothers bent on hating each other and trapping me in the middle.

TROUBLING SIGNS AHEAD

I could have blamed myself for our poor relationship. My own marriage was crumbling. Signs were everywhere. My wife Yahindi was perpetually angry with me for leaving dishes on the couch and forgetting to cap the toothpaste. She also didn't like my cats, their litter-box smell, hair on the carpet and their fleas. It all goes with cats, my joy.

She and I often prayed together, my way of peacefully ending our day. But even that did not ease our tension. When I displayed a crucifix and candle near the couch where I slept, she hid them. In her faith practice, there were no such artifacts - no crosses in their church or religious candles in their homes.

That may be because many Protestants believe that too much attention is given to symbols rather than God. Theologians argue that early Christians did not use such symbols. In other words, Yahindi's Protestantism could not cohabit with my Catholicism. Put simply, her dogma and mine could not get along. Our language difference was the major problem. I studied Spanish, becoming somewhat competent. But, Yahindi's native Spanish was so rapid, I could not understand it. Problems never got talked out. One of those problems was her Saturday nights outings with friends. Dressed in finery, she would leave the house, not returning until dawn. Relying on old defenses, I would think, "Isn't that nice that she has friends?" Often, she would take selfies in her evening wear before leaving me for the night.

I turned my attention to Leticia, heaping her with love and praise. That is why I scheduled her manicure, a Christmas gift. When I saw that she had removed the acrylic nails later that week, I asked, "What happened to them?" "I didn't like them," she replied.

I didn't believe it. Then, I found the new Christmas sweaters I had bought her mother. They were neatly stacked in my home office. Noted Eureka counselor Lewis Quinby would advise, "Listen for what they don't say." In this case, the silence was deafening.

LIFE WITH A GRINGO

Losing grip on Leticia was more painful than the breakup of my marriage. I wanted to be a father. I cried when I first dropped her off at school and again when she graduated into high school. She was a pain - as teenage daughters can be - but, I loved the abuse. I would wake our daughter and drive her to school, intent on embarrassing her along the way. I would sing hip-hop songs as we approached the school, rolling down the window to share my coolness. Embarrassed, she would dash from the car as I blew kisses. I loved it all, especially the night of her first school dance. I told her that I would stand by in case some unlucky kid made a move on her. I told her that the first kid who came to pick her up for a date would get my special treatment, my .38 revolver. Actually, marrying her off to a Catholic kid wouldn't be so bad.

At midnight, she would hand wash the dishes, crashing together pots and pans - a Dominican poltergeist. The sudden silence in the kitchen meant she was almost done. All that remained was the final volley, a pot dropped to the kitchen floor. In show business, they call it "jumping the shark." That was Fonzi's way of giving life to a dying "Happy Days" television series. Leticia's dish-washing was growing equally old.

My new wife was learning to hate me in two languages. Bilingual insults gave her two shots at me. And unlike the COVID vaccine, these shots were lethal. Nothing about me impressed her. What did she want from me, a trip to the Holy Lands? Yes, she did. So, in December of 2018, one year after she moved to California, I booked three tickets to Jerusalem, to celebrate the cradle of Christianity. There, the poor in spirit could replenish their faith for $10,000, airfare and hotel included.

I remember Yahindi and her daughter walking the shores of the Sea of Galilee and riding on the back of a Bedouin camel. I walked with them through the streets of Old Jerusalem and the Garden of Gethsemane. We stood on the banks of the Jordan River and watched joyful people baptized. Christmas Eve, we took a bus to Bethlehem in the Palestinian sector. As Yahindi and Leticia wandered through cobblestone streets, I puffed up the hill toward the Church of the Nativity, the place where Jesus was born. The square was crowded with tourists, all hoping for a glimpse of the Midnight Mass. We waited futilely in the cold. There was no room in the church, just as there had been none at the inn for Jesus' parents. Even in the most sacred place, things don't happen as we want. You would think that in 2000 years we would have learned that.

ENDURING LOVE

One year later, 2019, our own marriage was dissolving. I decided to divorce and start over. That would involve weeks of waiting and hours in crowded courtrooms. It happens all the time in Family Court as people bickered over children and money. Divorce seemed as routine as ordering pizza - without the food. I wanted a restraining order from Yahindi. Others wanted the same, their stories more complicated. One man wanted to know about child support for an unborn baby. "What if it is not my baby?" asked a man. I groaned, trapped in the "Maury Povich Show" with no mute button. Another wife had taken their child to live in England. He wanted her to pay for his plane ticket to visit the child and spend a few extra days touring London. In other words, he wanted a paid vacation. Even the Family Court judge was having problems, sued by a former Public Defender. The attorney alleged that the judge, drunk at a houseboat party, had tossed him into the lake while uttering anti-Semitic insults.

And I thought I had problems. Our final divorce hearing was by Zoom. I never saw Yahindi's face and heard only her voice, crisp and emotionless. I would never have a chance to ask what went wrong.

THINKING IT OVER

Without my wife and daughter, I spent my days and nights in pandemic silence. It was overwhelming. I sifted through old family photographs, baby pictures, weddings, and graduations. They stirred memories of my years as a family man. They had been successful though not sustainable. And for the next pandemic year, masked and afraid to leave my house, it did not appear that I would have another chance.

When I wasn't reminiscing, I was watching the TV news - a big mistake. Networks were beginning to report that the single diagnosed COVID 19 case in Washington was the tip of the iceberg. The virus was creeping across the country as doctors warned of an epidemic while government leaders were promising it would go away. None of this was reassuring to me. I struggled with chronic heart disease. More lung issues like COVID would kill me. That was certain. I began to see life in the past tense. I felt alone and frightened. My friends who had so often promised to help with shopping and house cleaning had moved on.

We all had a story to tell and no one to listen. My only outlet were the stories I could create without leaving home.I videotaped anything that moved. That included my cats licking each other and playing with my mail ordered toilet paper. I dug out my diecast car collection and began to order more. So any day's mail delivery could include a shiny new model Duesenberg just like the one *The Great Gatsby* would drive to his lavish parties. Now, that same sedan could tour my living room carpet, spinning wildly around my cat's hairballs. F. Scott Fitzgerald would have been proud. I also bought a miniature ambulance and surmised if I couldn't be revived, it required only that I fit into a two-inch coffin.

My garage yielded even more treasures. Among them were the films and tapes of my TV career. Watching these videos which were faded, scratched and muffled, brought it all back. Still, they reminded me of the life I led on my own - a three ring adventure circus. It was not so far removed from my sideshow student who ate worms and stapled paper to her head.

In Arcata Plaza with my best friend and side-kick Skip Bale

THE FAMILY GUY

My first wife, Lois, must have loved my joie de vivre. I recorded our adventures on 16 mm film. One of them was a scratchy documentary about a 1974 road trip to Newfoundland. We stayed with her Aunt Ita who hid bottles of liquor in her clothes dryer. While we toured the rugged coast, Ita would sit at home to drink. That was family as she saw it. My documentary was nothing I would have shown on TV, it was as riveting as my solid waste documentary but without the waste. I premiered it at one of our first house parties. Guests drank heavily and left early. My wife did not want kids and insisted that I be sterilized. She insisted that my vasectomy would show the world our concern for overpopulation. In other words, I would be doing the world a favor by not making another David. When our marriage fell apart, I was again a free agent, my curb appeal as a father somewhat diminished along with my sperm count.

On the second try, sperm count didn't matter. I married a dental hygienist and single mother to a seven year old girl. I had become a father, side stepping those years of diapers and midnight feedings. On the other hand, I was the one needing a burping. Susannah was the flower girl in the wedding at Cape Elizabeth Lighthouse, the entrance to Portland Harbor.

I recorded our honeymoon to Spain on 35 mm slides. We took a boat to Morocco to visit one of my ham radio friends. He promised us a ride on a "humpy" camel. He also kept his booze in his clothes dryer. I sensed a pattern here. He would take us on his liquor fueled drive through the Casbah, taking aim at "f---king red-hats," men in red fezzes. Thank God we didn't happen upon a Shriner's convention. Back home, I insisted on adopting Susannah. It was the only way I could continue the Silverbrand name, already synonymous with "felony," thanks to my brothers.

When she was 13, I took Susannah on a school trip to Russia. My colleague was a school teacher, William Forstchen, and we had co-sponsored a resolution in the Maine Legislature to encourage a U.S. Russia venture to Mars. We visited the Moscow Air and Space Museum. There, we met a U.S. astronaut and Russian cosmonaut.

President Ronald Reagan was already Cold War saber-rattling, and the Soviet government used our visit as a media counter-message. Americans didn't want nuclear war. The Russians had proof, a bedazzled TV reporter and a star-struck teacher from Maine.

Neither Forstchen, a student of World History, nor I, a student of complete sentences, could have predicted the media-play of our visit. That may explain Forstchen's fixation on the bank of Soviet news cameras awaiting our arrival.. With our students, we had suddenly become media fodder – or at least Forstchen did. He took his seat at the table with Russian dignataries while I watched from the sidelines. I was sure that in the midst of it all, Forstchen would jump to his feet and demand that I sit at his side. It was, after all, our collaboration as teacher and journalist that had gotten us this far, Forstchen's photo published world-wide by Associated Press.

It didn't happen. I had been left at the alter, so to speak, forgotten at a prime moment in our project. I was as crimson as the planet Mars, the significance of my help ignored. It swept over me like a nuclear winter and Forstchen's "I'm so sorry," didn't cover it back at the hotel.

In time we made up. But I missed the true meaning of our visit—what happened to my daughter Susannah, though she would never admit it. Her life changed course dramatically after that trip. Her visit visit with Russian kids may have opened her eyes to a career in diplomacy. At a Moscow school, they played a computer game through which countries at odds could resolve differences online. Point made, Russian kids serenaded U.S. students with an old civil rights song, "We Shall Overcome." That must have been the point at which Susannah chose her career path in international diplomacy. In high school, she was a U.S. Senate Page, nominated by Senate Majority Leader George Mitchell.

On C-Span, I could watch her on the U.S. Senate floor, darting from one senator's desk to another. On our visit to the Capitol, one senator pointed her out as his favorite page. He was the Junior Senator from Delaware, Joe Biden. Later, we visited with President George H.W. Bush in the Oval Office where my wife gave him a small stuffed moose from Maine. It was magical, the three of us sitting in that historic room, a White House photographer snapping our picture.

We appeared to be a forever family, graced with health and promise. What could go wrong? Everything, it turned out. In less than a year, she wanted a divorce. The news was broken to me by a Catholic marriage counselor. So much for those forever wedding vows. In breakups, memories don't count. It's all about numbers, the only gauge we seem to use. Property value, child support - these are the indices of marriage and divorce, the way we quantify it.

When my partner Nina died, her family reluctantly gave me cash and free use of a house as long as I lived. Our attorneys settled on my 10-year life expectancy. It is unsettling to believe that Nina's family would be richer when I died because then they could have their house back.

In the perfect world, people in love would file a flight plan. That way, if they had to ditch the aircraft, others would know where to look for them. My father, an amateur pilot, often failed to file a flight plan, winding up in deep trouble. Once, he flew from Visalia to Fresno for what he claimed was a school meeting. Fresno was blanketed in thick fog and pilots advised to avoid landing there. Pop ignored the advice and overshot the runway, rolling to a stop in a muddy field. He grabbed his briefcase, rolled up his pants and walked barefoot to the nearest farmhouse. Seeing him, a barefooted man in a business suit, was too much for the woman who answered the door. She screamed and slammed it shut. Meanwhile, airport investigators were looking for the plane that disappeared from radar. They stopped my father and asked if he had seen it. He pointed to the muddy field and then kept walking in the other direction. Moments later, the airport investigators returned and asked my father if he knew anything about the abandoned plane. "Yes, I do," he replied as they ordered him into the car. His life on the run was over, at least for now.

Lovers take off over the ocean of love without a backup plan, let alone life jackets. They are unprepared for foul weather. Rescued at sea, they'll board another plane to make the same mistakes. Divorced from Catherine in 1992, I was ready to try a lifelong relationship again, this time with a flight plan.

LIFE IN 16 MM

Nina was a military widow, her husband had left money to start her own care home business. That was her sole income the winter of 1992, when I rolled into town with all I owned in a U-Haul trailer. To be sure, I was an odd man, collector of old radios and baseball memorabilia. I also had my portfolio of 16 mm news stories from Maine. I was a consummate storyteller, sharing accounts of my old reporting days. They were told in soft monotone with no finite point. Having bored myself, I would abruptly end them with, "But I got through that one alright."

Once, I almost ran over a roller skater with a Ford Model A. It happened in a Portland, Maine Fourth of July parade in which I was assigned to drive the car, the roller skater towed behind. Confused by its gas and brake levers, I nearly drove into a junior high school baton twirling team. Panicking, I flipped the car in reverse, nearly backing over the skater. But I got through that one alright. I knew as little about life's gas and brake levers, coasting into Eureka in a rusty Subaru. Looking as gaunt as a P. O.W., concerned Nina's 80-year-old mother who asked, "Is he okay?" Not really. That is why I had enrolled in a small, local dating service, a sort of no kill shelter for abandoned men. I could have used a flea bath and brushing.

So began the legacy of my life with Nina and her best friend, Jone Kosack. You can't choose your family but you can, your friends. In Jone, she found a guardian angel. Nina met her at the cosmetics counter at Gottshalk's, a Bayshore Mall department store. I knew Jone was a closer. When I wanted to apply a woman's makeup for a TV feature, she recruited the store manager for my experiment. When I expressed interest in Nina, Jone demanded "What are your intentions?" Jone was the woman you wanted on your side. Until I came into the picture, the only other men Nina had been close to were the muscle bound dancers she saw at a nightclub one evening. They were the loincloth clad Australians, who brought their "down unders" precariously close to Nina. From that view alone, I was a significant product downgrade.

Still, my persistence grew on her. Soon, she and I were officially engaged, a union that lasted until her death 20 years later. Nina liked Lincoln Continentals, gunning hers around town, her head barely visible above the steering-wheel. She and I would dine in Eureka's nightspots, nestling in the corner with crab salads and conversation. Talk usually revolved around my boss, the demonic manager of the TV station. She didn't like me because she didn't like anybody. It must have been hard for Nina to endure my complaints. When she complained to my mother about my caterwauling, Mom replied, "I know. He does that a lot."

Soon I was complaining about Nina's kids, unable to let us lead our own lives. Her son, for example, seemed to fail at every scheme he tried, travel consulting, real estate investment counseling and even marriage. When he failed, he would return to Nina to recuperate. I took my complaints to a family counselor, a silver-haired woman with homespun wisdom. "So you're stuck in a shitstorm," she said. Indeed I was, and the counselor's advice haunts me still. "Given the choice between her son or you," warned the woman, "she'll choose her son. Deal with it." And so I did for 20 years.

Nina and I would gambol in the streets of London and Paris while her son, living with us by then, kept an eye on things at home, her jewelry and my cameras - anything of cash value. "I hope you guys have a wonderful time," he would say as we left on another trip. I knew he surely would. In the pandemic year, Jone Kosack was the one voice I could count on, the daily voice on the phone. We all need that. With each call, Jone would cut to the chase. "Start talkin'" she would say as I would spew out my stories of love and loss. We shared love with Nina and grief when she was gone. Now I was sure that Nina was still watching me "try to behave." Now, Jone was her earthly deputy. Without parental guidance, I needed that. Sometimes quoting her former family counselor, Lewis Quinby, sometimes from her own experience, Jone would be brutally blunt - but rarely wrong. Every phone call would terminate with, "Keep me in the know."

NINA'S DEATH

Jone helped me survive May 1, 2013, the day so much changed. That was the day Nina died in the crosswalk near our house. She had been walking out Bichon Frise dog before heading off to her care home for the day. She was struck and killed by a truck owned by a U.S. Postal Service contractor, Timothy McTague. He had been headed to Blue Lake on an early morning mail run when he turned the corner at the intersection near our house. She was in the crosswalk of that intersection. She died instantly when he hit her though not cited by police. They chalked it up as "one of those things."

We were all left abandoned, becoming bitter rivals. They were fearful that I would steal her money. I was afraid I would be homeless and penniless. Gone were the days through which we had so much fun. Fourth-of-July was my favorite. In our kitchen, Nina's 80-year-old mother, Harmony, would mix sugar, sauce and her special supplements into a giant tub, blending them by hand. At the Eureka Fourth of July Festival, we would sell those meat sticks for the hundreds who would stand in line. I was the designated cashier, stuffing bills into a cash box to be counted and divided later at home. That was Nina's mother's favorite time, watching me sort and stack the bills, writing down the amounts. My first year with that stand, the family netted $4000, all of which Nina gave to the family. "Oh, gee, Mom," I didn't earn that much," her kids would say. But they always took it. Then a week later, we would drive to Reno to pump the cash into slot machines. That was Nina's family, playing, then working - then playing some more. It was an endless cycle of cash flow, with Nina at its core, her family floundering to find its way without parental guidance.

The first chance I got, I went rogue. When Nina died. I hitchhiked to the funeral rather than ride with the family. Five years later, a single-vehicle fatality brought those memories back. I was sad the day I learned of the fatality just outside Eureka. Driving alone, south of Eureka, Timothy McTague, lost control of his truck and struck a trailer. Police said speed was a factor. McTague was the driver of the truck that killed Nina.

LIFE ALONE

With Jone's help, I wrangled my way through NIna's estate settlement. Through months of litigation, I got to live rent-free in the house she and I had occupied in Cutten. It was a comfortable though lonely place, my shelter for as long as I lived and with whomever I lived. It was my shelter during the pandemic as I got to know its every ceiling crack and cobweb. In the bathroom, I would watch spiders dart around my bare feet and skirt for cover when my cats came hunting. We were friends, the insects and I, needing each other in this time of coexistence. Without them, I would have nothing to watch, only the endless litany of pandemic TV reports. I grew tired of smoke screens and scapegoats. I could also remember those nights when Jone would come over with husband John. We would start a fire in the fireplace and listen to oldies on my stereo, passing the night in laughter. I could hold those memories forever.

She helped me to accept my brother - a paid assassin - as a flawed human being, satisfied by getting away with something. In youth, it was the chocolate crumbs in the principal's office. Later, he would trick the telephone company to make free long distance calls. Detonating bombs in an orchard, Peter would savor the rush of the explosion. He said it was like seeing the face of God. So, it was not a stretch to think that his gun silencers and assassination manuals would inspire him without consequence.

I also could love him, but add others to my virtual family. People like Jone. I had always prayed for a sister, the spirit of Judith Claire. She was our parents' first born, dying of pneumonia at her sixth month. My mother never recovered from that, keeping her ashes in a cardboard urn. My younger brother buried those ashes in the backyard after our mother's death so no one else could have them. Later, our father tried to retrieve the remains, sifting soil from the burial site. There seemed no end to my family's strange concept of grief. Jone would teach me two things that got me through the pandemic. The first was that family could be whatever I wanted it to be. I could pick brother's and sisters and love them just as much. The second is that I could choose those things that brought me joy. I could feed the hungry while my brother was dropping cake crumbs and my wife was hiding my religious artifacts.

When my brother told me more about his crimes, I visited a man to whom I had given my car. His daughter Zoe had almost died four years ago, victim of a birth defect. When she was born, her stomach was outside her body. It took months of surgery to fix it. When my car broke down, mechanics claimed it was beyond repair. I gave it to Zoe's father, a construction worker. In a month, he had rebuilt the engine. For that, Zoe, a beautiful 4-year old, kissed me on the cheek. To me, that - not Peter's bomb - was the face of God. Maybe, by some grand design, I was able to make peace while Peter could not.

THE END OF DAYS - FILM AT 11.

Conspiracy theorists were predicting "The End" and recommended stockpiling food, ammunition and toilet paper. I was prepared to live off Shredded Wheat Cereal and frozen senior meals from the Blue Lake Rancheria. I still had chickpea soup, Salisbury steak and vegetables from when I was homebound two years ago with a heart condition. Now, those meals had fossilized like Ice Age relics. I was afraid to eat them. But if insurrectionists threatened me, I would have something lethal to shoot back.

In my solitude, I began to ponder nature's wonders. How would the cat on my back fence know that Princesa, my Persian Longhair kitten, was in heat? But he did, telling every stray in my neighborhood that there was fresh "fur" in town. How could they objectify her that way? Had they never heard of the "Meow Too Movement?" That was the worst of it - stumbling on a good joke and having no one to hear it. If one told a joke in a forest and no one heard it, would that make it unfunny? So, I would stash my jokes away until I had "Time Enough at Last." That was the "Twilight Zone" episode in which Burgess Meredith, a timid bank clerk, longs for time to read the classics. Then, when the earth is annihilated by a nuclear blast, he finds himself on the steps of a library surrounded by books. There, he breaks his glasses, unable to read. I knew the feeling, losing my glasses in the couch. Archaeologists will find them in the ruins of my house....

When I could venture out again, I found joy in annoying people. My video camera made it easy. The best way to enjoy life was to annoy people. And with my little video camera, I found many opportunities. Once, I stopped at a drive-thru coffee shop where the baristas wore bikinis. I had never before thought of stopping there. The idea was so unseemly. But to annoy someone, I would give it a shot. Camera rolling, I drove up to order a latte. The young woman covered her chest and ducked into a corner, a "Gotcha" moment in the "60 Minutes" tradition. As a teenager, I could have explained it the way I justified water ballooning lovers on Lookout Point. I said then that it was a moral imperative. But now I was a 70 year old man with better things to do - like taking my own blood pressure.

I struck again at the home of a Eureka guinea pig farmer. He had hundreds of these critters in his home, kept there because he couldn't find suitable homes for them. I tried unsuccessfully for days to visit him. Then, one Sunday, I saw a city Animal Control truck parked at his house. I saw an opportunity for breaking news: "Hundred Detained in Guinea-pig Round-up." I got my camera and tiptoed through his back yard until I found the pen where he kept them. "I'll bet there would be a journalism award in this for me," I thought. The guinea pigs had grown since I last saw them, similar to the Capybara of South America, the world's largest rodent. That must have been how menacing I appeared to the young Animal Control officer cleaning up the pen. She disappeared into the house, then stormed out into the yard ordering me off the property. "I'm sure it would be okay with the man if I were here," I offered. "Stop recording and leave now!" she ordered.

Of course she was right. I had no right to be there. It was one thing to videotape a transient in Arcata Plaza. It was another to trespass on someone's property to video a guinea pig colony. I empathized with the officer. She likely had to determine the gender of hundreds of guinea pigs. I'm not sure how one does that - but I wouldn't want the job. How would you do that, by questionnaire? In both cases, the coffee shop and the guinea pig farm, I had affirmed my mission - annoying people, as important to me as informing them. That was life as I had chosen to live it, a productive day, if not a reproductive one. I wasn't born an Annoying Silverbrand. I earned it.

LIFE ALONE: SOLITARY REFINEMENT

I adjusted to life alone, poisoning ant caravans as they rooted through cupboards looking for something edible. If the ants didn't like the food, I probably wouldn't either. I didn't look good in underwear, but I deserved the right to parade around in it to my heart's content.

I remember schooling a burly construction worker on that topic. He was working on power company transformers when I decided to take his picture. It was just after 9/11 and he told me that my video could be used by Al Qaeda to cripple our country. I said I had a First Amendment right to take his picture." Anything I can see from a public right of way can be photographed, even your private parts," I said. The man glared at me, obviously uncomfortable with my reference to his body. It annoyed him. Once again, I had accomplished my mission.

TROPICAL STORM

My thirst for adventure got me into trouble with a capital "Caribbean." The warm waters of lust had seduced Humphrey Bogart and Lauren Bacall. "You know how to whistle, don't you Steve?" she cooed in the film, *To Have and Have Not*... "Just put your lips together and blow." That sounded like fun to me, so I courted a Caribbean woman I found on a dating website, Yahindi, the woman I married after Nina's death. Yahindi lived and worked in Santiago, the Dominican Republic, employed by a church after school program.

I was sure she could find a similar job in Eureka. It didn't bother me that within days of our engagement, she quit her job. Later, we were legally married in a Santo Domingo strip mall and corresponded for the next four years while U.S. Homeland Security dealt with her visa. Each call from her usually involved a money request, more each time. Suddenly, I was saddled with debt as I bought her a refrigerator, bed and other furnishings. Through no fault of hers, everything there cost at least twice what it would in the U.S. In other words, you could put your lips together and "blow" a lot of dough in no time. I was sure that having them with me would be cheaper in my rent free home. So I sent them plane tickets and they were on their way. On a cold December night, the two landed in San Francisco and two days later, we headed north to Humboldt. We would be retracing the migration of many a pioneer, seeking freedom in open space and, for some, good weed. She cried as we crossed the Golden Gate Bridge and again when she saw a flock of sheep south of Fortuna. They represented the wool being pulled over my eyes.

We were settling into idyllic Humboldt life and blazing a new trail of love. Specifically, the trail ran off a farm road and nearly killed me. It happened on a driving lesson I gave her two weeks after her arrival. I had chosen the farm road so she could practice steering and accelerating, much as I had done with the Ford Model A in the Maine parade. This time it wasn't the roller skater in danger but me. When she took the wheel of my Honda Civic, she panicked and stomped on the gas pedal.The car veered off the road, through a barbed wire fence and into bushes. It shattered the windshield and caved in the roof. A branch shot over the dashboard and stopped inches from my chest. She wept as I gasped for air. The lesson was over, the car crumpled like a rose petal. She was unhurt while I suffered scrapes and bruises. EMT's extracted me from the wreckage. I forgave her, of course. It was just another bump in love's roadway. She asked for another lesson but I told her it would have to wait. I couldn't afford a new car.

We settled into wedded bliss with me in the driver's seat, driving Leticia to and from school and my wife to English classes. I worked part-time at the TV station while substitute teaching. I thought that my shortness of breath was just due to life's ups and downs, but it was worse. My heart and lungs were working too hard - "Congestive Heart Failure." I was coughing and stumbling around the office. "If someone else doesn't take you to the hospital, I will," she said.

THE SUMMER OF 2019

After a hospital battery of heart tests, I was admitted for three days of enemas, laxatives and diuretics, a virtual process of elimination I called "Club Med(s)." By my release date, I was pale and bloated, a human dirigible Hindenburg headed for a rough landing. Over the summer in my house, home health nurses poked and prodded me while I learned to use a walker. I wore diapers because I could not get to the bathroom fast enough while Leticia complained of the around-the-clock oxygen machine. I felt perpetually embarrassed and unclean, hooked to the plastic oxygen tube jammed up my nose. It was old age arriving way ahead of schedule. My doctor, though "healthful," was not helpful. He had my driver's license suspended and questioned my cognition.

For company, I would chat with imaginary people in my sleep. And with Ambien, I turned day into night and vice versa. For attention, I would trip over my oxygen tube and fall, once ripping the towel rack out of the wall as I landed between the sink and toilet. I'd fall a dozen times that summer, each with style, grace - and a hard landing. Once, I fell at the hospital, landing halfway out the exit. Security guards and nurses fought over my corpse. Inside the building, I was the nurse's responsibility. Outside was security guard territory. As they argued over me, I screamed for a taxi cab, escaping before they resolved the issue.

LAST FAMILY CHRISTMAS

I knew I needed to work again. My family needed the money and I needed reassurance. Reporting was the only thing I knew. With my old station reluctant to take me back, I considered other options. With Christmas approaching, I applied to be a Salvation Army bellringer. I would have been good at it too, bellowing "Merry Christmas" while clapping the bell, both within my skill set. My late grandmother, an old Salvation Army officer, would have been proud of me. In the name of Jesus, she had hauled many a drunk from a tavern for a soulful blast from my grandfather's cornet.

I also applied to another TV station as a news producer. I knew the lingo and loved the fast-paced life of TV news in the country's smallest media market. Car into a light pole? Bank robber fleeing with an undisclosed amount of cash? I could handle it all, gasping from one fallen tree limb to another with my small video camera. When Loleta Cheese Factory had a meltdown, I was all over it like cheddar in a cheese sandwich. The station asked me to do a live shot from Loleta. I still had my chops from all those live shots in Maine. From Election night to New Year's Eve - I had covered them all. And they still talked about my live coverage of the ozone over the Atlantic.

We set up our live gear, just as I had for so many breaking stories in Maine. Now, 30 years later, I was shivering with excitement beneath a hot TV light. Behind me was the mournfully empty shelf where the cheese spread had been. The Eureka station KAEF had made a gutsy move when it pulled me off the respirator for another shot at the news. My boss, News Director, Nazy Javid screamed gleefully when she heard my name on the intercom.

On the home-front, nothing was okay. I was losing grip on my marriage and my wife told me she didn't love me anymore. Our upcoming Christmas dinner would be our last together. "I want all this to happen with joy and peace," she wrote. "Enjoy this wonderful opportunity God gives us to share together." I spooned an extra helping of turkey stuffing. I returned to work sobbing. Marissa, the evening producer, sent me back home. She had known me in happier times. She was my former Journalism student at College of the Redwoods. At the Arcata satellite campus, I felt frisky and free. I could keep my distance from those dour English teachers who questioned my "pedagogy," whatever that meant. Maybe it was the way I had run the student newspaper, The Corsair. In a freewheeling but pointless essay, one of my students had referred to "f---ing Quakers." I didn't know about it until the paper was published, a reader referring sarcastically to the "nice Quaker reference." I was livid, asking the writer about his language use. "I just thought it was cool," he responded. I dashed out to retrieve all Corsair editions, black marking every Quaker reference.

Then there was a recovered heroin addict, "Horse," who often spoke in unintelligible rants. In my class, he learned to write them out, publishing his own edition of the campus paper, "The Horsehair." In general, students didn't know the difference. Honestly, they had a point. In Arcata, I had taken Marissa's class to Arcata Plaza, where wanderers often gathered. I planned to teach my students about "Gonzo Journalism," the freewheeling Hunter S. Thompson style. His drug-fueled articles changed the nature of modern Journalism. To the "Who, What, When, Where and How" approach, he had added "What the hell?" I was about to show students my power of friendly professionalism, "Gonzo Journalism" with compassion.

Arcata Plaza would be my blank canvas. "Go screw yourself!" shouted the man on the bench, flipping me off. "This is a public park," I responded. "Screw you," he shouted back. "Grow up," I retorted. He jumped to his feet lunging toward me, "I'll take that camera and...," he shouted. I wasn't ready for a Sony suppository. One of my students led me away. I made my job look so easy. Marissa was doing well on her own. She had asked a young transient what he liked about Arcata Plaza. "I would rather be here than have Hep C," he told her. Actually, you could have both.

Their final project was to prove their chops as investigative journalists. One group tackled a burning question, "Could one still be productive on 100 blunts of weed a day?" That was musician Bob Marley's claim and my group wanted to verify it. In a farmhouse, where one of them lived, they piled weed on a kitchen table and began rolling joints. They smoked as they worked, jotting down their observations. Their inquiry went up in smoke. An hour into their experiment, they decided that they didn't care. They switched to a related topic, llama herding.

Years later, I encountered one of my students, a public defender, in the courthouse. She "bluntly" denied the story. Other students had shown similar passion, one for earthworms which she swallowed as a circus act. Kat also swallowed light bulbs and stapled documents to her head, all to adoring crowds. I admired her passion and promised to see her perform. One Saturday night, she appeared on stage in a leather tutu. It was my proudest professional moment, my student finding a vocation so similar to my own. In class the next week, I found Kat leaning over a wastebasket. "I don't feel so good," she groaned. "Of course you don't, honey." I replied. "You eat worms."

SOME PEOPLE SAY I'M CRAZY, BUT I'M NOT THE ONLY ONE

Years later at the last Christmas feast, my Dominican wife could have served worms and I wouldn't have known the difference. My senses were dead along with my heart. Fire crackled in our fireplace, its light dancing on the Christmas ornaments. Leticia and her mother lightly bantered in Spanish as I cried over my meal. I groped for something positive to make of it all. The turkey stuffing was scrumptious. So many times, I have revisited life's seminal moments - the good and the bad. I used my time on pandemic lockdown to do that. I have tried when possible to reconnect with the people I loved so as to learn from my mistakes. Sure, I had sometimes made a mess of things, spilling molasses on the floor of my life. A little boy had done that to W. C. Fields' general store in the movie The clerk replied, "I told him, I wouldn't do that if I were you."

In my year alone, I spread a lot of "molasses" on the floor, none as colorful as my friendship with Sandra, the restless spirit of South Fortuna. Living alone, Sandra drove her neighbors crazy with nighttime cursing and reckless drives through the neighborhood. She graffitied her own sidewalk and hung witches and skeletons on her trees and a dead owl on her back fence. Neighbors complained to police whose frequent responses changed nothing. To neighbors, she was clearly out of control and a danger to their children. They said as much through frequent phone calls to my TV station. I visited the neighborhood to document their complaints, Sandra driving by and yelling unintelligibly.

I decided to pay her a midnight visit as only I could. Her lights were on when I arrived, pajama wearing neighbors milling about. Cautiously, I approached the front door and called out. No response. Then, I left a bouquet of flowers, told her I loved her and walked away. The flowers changed everything. On a subsequent visit, she was wearing underwear she described as a bathing suit. She professed her love for Vladimir Putin, but said that she also liked me. As for the dead owl, she said she had found it by the side of the road and hung it on the fence as a memorial.

Sure, there seemed no sense to Sandra. That's why Humboldt County Mental Health Department workers intervened and locked her down for observation. She told me that for two days, psychiatrists tried to give her medication she did not want. After her release, she went away, destination undisclosed. Her neighborhood was eerily quiet. Perhaps I had violated professional ethics by giving her the flowers. I am sure the neighbors would not have approved. Nor would they have endorsed my plan to take her out for coffee - as long as she wore clothes. I would do it again the same way, chalking it up to one misunderstood old person to another. It is the kind of person I had always been, but more so in the year of the pandemic. Who defined crazy? And once defined, what would they do about it? "I wouldn't do that if I were you," someone would have advised me about Sandra and the flowers. But I would "do that" every chance I could.

VISION IN KNEELAND

Lots of people claimed Kneeland as a holy place. On a hill overlooking Eureka, Kneeland was a piece of unspoiled paradise, home to farm animals and the off-grid people who tended to them. It was also home to a transmitter site, a building holding the firepower for local broadcast stations. From a giant tower, their antennas spewed the broadcast material that defined us as a culture, soap operas, game shows and the Super Bowl. For the big game, we had hired security guards to handle angry mobs in the event the transmitter failed. The transmitter was also refuge for broadcast chief engineers maintaining the circuitry while also sheltering in place from the wrath of the boss, the station manager.

One manager for whom I worked was so autocratic, his chief engineer would disappear for days, explaining he was working on transmitter problems "up on Kneeland." Whenever he announced he was "headed to Kneeland," we knew he was in the doghouse with the boss and was looking for a hiding place. Dirty windows at the TV studio? Time to go to the transmitter. Boss cranky from a weekend bender? Time to head to Kneeland. It became our chief engineer's second home. Unfortunately, that included a surrogate spouse away from home as well. The engineer had taken up with a younger woman. With sleeping quarters, Kneeland was the perfect place for romance and for fine-tuning those final amplifiers.

The experience was as electrifying as finding an exotic mushroom. Even Humboldt County mushroom gatherers knew that. Once they had tried to kick me out of a mushroom convention at Redwood Acres Fairgrounds. Enthusiasts from all over had brought their plants to compete in the "Best of Show Sporophore" competition. Experts marveled over the fungi as they labeled them by type. They muttered approval as they jotted notes. I sensed their awe and wonderment. I began taking video of the judging, moving in for close shots as the experts ignored me. Then, a mushroom collector huffed, "You will have to leave. You're interfering." "I'm almost done." That was not good enough. He repeated his order, ignoring my plea that I was only trying to publicize the show. He began yelling at me as I stomped toward my car. "Don't ever expect me to cover your mushroom club again," I yelled. "Get out of here!" he yelled. "And I won't be back anytime soon," I retorted. I had done it again, scorching the earth where once blades of hope had been, standing my ground for no good reason. Other journalists had been jailed for defiant truth. I would forever mark my reputation as the man who "harshed" the mushroom collectors.

FACING THE FIRST COVID CASE

"COVID is here," said the young reporter across the TV news-room. Humboldt County had just recorded its first virus case and I dashed to the County Health Department for more information. My first question would be "What is a COVID?" It couldn't wait. Maybe the story would fizzle, as so many Humboldt happenings did. We are masters of almost news. The previous Thanksgiving, my boss Nazy had discovered a fully cooked turkey lying in the middle of a major highway. She had the video, steam still emanating from the turkey's breastplate - a full-course family meal lying in the passing lane. From what oven had it flown the coop? I'd spent my career covering "almost" news. Remember, I'd gone live covering Loleta's last grilled cheese sandwich.

Of course, the virus was all too real, changing me in ways I could not imagine. I was lucky to be a loner, growing up as my own best playmate. Shy and awkward outside my own bubble, the government "stay-at-home" order didn't bother me as much as it did others. I was home alone most of the time anyway. My cats loved it - more time with Daddy and less time preening. They would sleep with me, cuddling into the curves of my body. They also got along well together, washing each other's faces and cuddling near my space heater. It was the kind of information I shared only with intimate friends. Two many details and I might appear as the third lover in a triangle.

I had known other animal lovers, their obsession enormously disturbing. One was a supermarket cashier, Jerry, who collected tropical birds. You couldn't buy a quart of milk at Jerry's register without his lecture on the latest bird in his collection. "Have you heard of the Costa Rican Cockatiel?" Jerry would gush as he sorted through his photographs on the register. It was easy to see that Jerry's rants were not endearing him with customers. When Jerry did not appear one day, we knew that management had had enough. They had banished him. But like the carrier pigeon, he always came back. We found him at another supermarket down the street, the same stack of bird photos and gushing enthusiasm. He died when he fell from his office chair, a freak home accident. Animal advocate Shannon Miranda rescued the birds while he found them new homes. Any day, one could walk through the bird cages of Shannon's animal rescue farm. Riled by one's presence, birds would screech. I knew the feeling.

Trapped in my own pandemic cage for the next year, I felt like opening my beak for a blood-curdling yell. Jerry helped me to better understand my soulmate Ed Kirkpatrick, the old man who had spread his mother's ashes on my news camera. It happened on his land parcel just off Broadway in Eureka. A retired landscaper, Ed owned the parcel establishing a transient camp. "All they need is a second chance," he would say. And the transients would return to camp with bicycles, chainsaws and power tools, items they claimed to have found on their morning walks. They had found a source cheaper than those discount hardware stores. They just took stuff. Ed was a holdover hippie whose years of dreaming had left him a penniless target for needy people. And they knew it. Still, I admired his dreams, nurtured on the streets of Haight-Ashbury. So I stood in the rain that day as Ed scattered his mother's ashes. A gust of wind caught them, blowing them back on my news camera, covering it with gray powder. Back at work. I euphorically walked through the office. "Hey, what's that shit on your camera?" a coworker asked me. Oh," I replied. "It's just some guy's mom." Twice, Eureka Police had dismantled camps Kirkpatrick had permitted. Transients were wounded souls in Ed's eyes, and like the cockatiels of Costa Rica, they needed protection.

That put him at odds with a number of city health and safety codes and the people who enforced them. He was annoying people in record numbers, which is why I liked him. If you didn't annoy someone every day, I believed, you weren't trying hard enough. I can thank the pandemic for finally finding Ed one day. I had nothing to do and nowhere to go. I was lonely and bored, susceptible to the latest scandal on the national news. Ed was seated in his easy chair, surrounded by juice bottles, his long white hair and beard askew. Ed told me he hadn't been down to the lot, now denuded of brush, artifacts, shipping containers and the people who lived in them. "If you were divorced from your wife, would you want to see her again?" he asked. I had to agree. I had survived another pandemic day exploring my past, the child who sought strange playmates and talked to himself. I still had the same camera I had used the day he scattered the ashes - and the feeling that Ed's mother was in its crevices.

WHAT I LEARNED FROM EMILY DICKINSON

Without the reclusive New England poet, I might not have survived the pandemic - not emotionally. She was the nineteenth-century poet who defined the power of words. She wrote beautifully of flies and spiders, elegance in ordinary things.

I began to create video narratives about life at home, creating scenes with my die-cast car models, just as I had as a child. They were police dramas, squad cars cornering fugitives and an ambulance to pick up the wounded. In another made-for-TV drama, I staged a publication party for my book *"Dave's House"* and dressed as F. Scott Fitzgerald, *The Great Gatsby* author. In my fantasy story, his Duesenberg sedan was blocking my driveway.

My boss ran my stories on the news, but I could tell she was sometimes hesitant. "Just keep track of your hours," she would say. I got the same reaction with my cat story. I said that I had been licking my paws and hunting for fleas. I could spend hours wondering how fleas would know where to bite my cats. Their tiny blood sport? Maybe fleas were smarter than we realized. My ants were using coded messages, they could tell each other where I had discarded something sweet, a cupcake, hamburger wrapper or drop of orange juice. In minutes, they would send caravans of foot soldiers - insurrectionists - feasting in my trash.

LAST VISIT?

My brother Peter loved these stories. Before the COVID lockdown, I would share them in the visiting room of the Stockton Healthcare Facility where he lived. Approaching 80, his eyesight and health failing, he had been sent to spend the rest of his days at the hospital prison. Alone, I would drive the six hours to see him, spending the night in a motel in a sketchy section of the city. In the morning, I would wait in the visiting center with other families as corrections officers checked my credentials. Then, in the heat of the San Joaquin Valley morning, I would walk across the long courtyard to see him.

**With my brother Peter at California Department
of Corrections Stockton Healthcare Facility**

I knew to bring pockets of quarters for the vending machines there. Tired of prison food, Peter loved ice cream and candy. Because I was always short on cash, my own menu consisted of free condiments on a nearby table. Mixing mayonnaise, ketchup and barbecue sauce, I could create a zesty soup. His favorites stories were those of dust-ups with other inmates, lifers with walkers. As the inside joke went "I'm old. Don't mess with me. Another life sentence won't stop me from hurting you."

One of my brother's friends, Madison, suffered from a severe bipolar disorder. He had also been shot in the head with a .357 magnum pistol. The bullet had entered and exited his skull, damaging his already fragmented thinking. As a result, Madison would often explode in temper tantrums, shouting expletives, some targeting my brother. "Why don't you rough him up?" Peter's friends would ask. But my brother wouldn't. To him, Madison was just having a rough day. Once, Madison shoved Peter and he fell to the ground, striking his head on cement. He awoke in a hospital room recovering from a concussion. Peter's fellow inmates vowed to settle the score for him, whether or not he approved. In the exercise yard, Madison, a Latino, got roughed up by Black inmates. "Prison justice," Peter explained. Black inmates had waited to see if whites would stand up for Peter... When they didn't, the Black inmates got the "job" done. That was prison justice Peter saying he would miss his visits with Madison, expletives and all. "Why not just forgive him?" I asked. "That's not the way it works here," said Peter.

That was not so far from the way it worked in Peter's outside world. There, people paid a deadly price for disloyalty. Peter had seen to that. When it comes to his health, rules don't apply. Contracting prostate cancer a decade ago, he suffered while prison doctors did little until it was too late. It metastasized, spreading to his bones. With the COVID lockdown, I would not be able to see him, our visits limited to 15-minute phone calls. He rarely spoke about his cancer, preferring to talk about NASCAR and politics. I had to accept that with Peter's loss, I would be further isolated from my family.

THE UNINVITED CO-CONSPIRATOR

My younger brother still harbored rage about his mother's remains and how it took Peter's lawsuit to get them back. In retaliation, my younger brother disinvited me from his son's wedding. Nina had insisted we go anyway. Family and friends gathered at a Calistoga winery for the ceremony. As my younger brother glared at me, I sipped wine and toasted the couple.

"Maybe," I thought, "He had matured and we could bury our differences." Hoping so, I sent him a card that holiday wishing him "Seasons Greetings." "What do you mean by that," he responded.

He didn't realize how much I had envied him through the years, his rugged good looks and sense of adventure. With a smile, my younger brother could sweep women off their feet, even our mother's teacher friends at afternoon tea. Once enraptured, they would abandon home and husbands for wild romps in San Francisco. My other brother, Peter had that attraction too. These were the 1960's when cultural norms were changing, my wild brothers benefiting from that change.

Now, time and health were the great equalizers, debilitating those who once roamed free in the Garden of Eden. Knees were wearing out, hair turning gray, and it was time for baby boomers to take stock of the life that remained. They needed time to do that and, for all its calamity, the pandemic gave us that time. Through my pandemic, people I knew were accepting and joyful of the life they still had. They said they had never been happier and I agreed. Furthermore, hate is hard work. It requires energy and memory. For my younger brother, it demanded recollection of dates, times and names, every hurt cataloged for future reference. Otherwise, how awkward it would be to demand, "Remind me why I hate you." With my fading memory, I wouldn't be much help.

On a trip to California one year, I budgeted my time between my two brothers and separated parents, certain it had been equally divided. It had not, and for ten years, they squabbled over that one West Coast week. My mother's burial issue at least gave them something more substantial. Incarcerated for life, Peter was the first to admit his flaws and how they hurt his family. He regretted his drug and gun activity in our mother's house. Now he wanted simply to live without pain and see clearly the cement corridors of his home.

LEGACY OF MY BROTHERS

For better or worse, these were my brothers' gifts to me - the memories we had shared. With Peter, at least, we talked about the life he could have led and the one he chose. I would have to accept the lives he had taken. Given the time, I would retrace his trek through the mountains of Mexico, visiting the people he knew if they were still living. I would follow his path to the Mexican border where his pot laden Ford Fairlane slipped through security. On another trip, I would drive to Reno to seek out the old importer of illegal machine guns, convicted with his wife of that crime. I would ask him about the bargain he struck with Peter and how a federal informant against him was executed.

Some stories are better left alone, but accepting them has helped me to heal. It has also helped me to enrich the role I have played in others' lives. I learned that love is more important than familial titles with which we are burdened. I will always be a brother to Peter, and even to my younger brother, still estranged. I was a father to Nina's son, whose drug addiction took him before he was 50. I was father to Susannah, though I have tried to show her that titles do not matter. She will always be my friend, the petulant young woman who taught me to ride horses and behave so admirably in Russia and Washington D.C. Some day, when she is ready, she will tell me about her Middle East adventures in the U.S. Foreign Service and how she became the mother of two beautiful children.

I'LL CALL YOU MY FATHER

In the pandemic, I found a silver lining even in the Dominican marriage that had gone horribly wrong. Brian, Yahindi's son, was living alone there, left to deal with depression and isolation. When we first met in Santiago, I had bought him a school uniform. The dawn of his first day in class, Brian rose to iron it.

Now an adult, he was pursuing a career in media, though jobs on the island were hard to find. To me, the Caribbean would always be a demonic place where one could lose his money and his heart. Maybe one day I could give love another chance there. But not now.

Brian had reached out to me, sometimes calling me at midnight. I would listen to him and make him laugh. He said I was the father he always wanted. We all deserve that one good thing.

TWO SHOTS TO GO

The sun was setting over the Kneeland mountain. Across the snow covered valley, the moon was emerging from a cloud-bank. Reporter Marissa and I had gone there,1000 feet above Eureka, for a live shot about the weather for our evening news. There in the falling light, I felt a heavenly presence. The moon was comforting me.

Back home alone that night, my phone rang. A nurse from my hospital was offering a COVID vaccine the next morning, my first. I thought about the miracle of it all, a deadly virus wiping out much of the world population. And within a calendar year, researchers had found at least three vaccines to stave it off. Someone who passed science classes I flunked had developed a life-saving compound. Now, my name was on a list to receive it. The next morning, I barely felt the jab as the nurse squeezed the vaccine into my shoulder. Then, I sat for 15 minutes to make certain I would not have a bad reaction. It doesn't restore my youth. A pacemaker still keeps me alive. Still, it changes the way I look at life.

That afternoon, I bought ten fully cooked, rotisserie chickens and passed them out to homeless drug addicts near the waterfront. They didn't bother with paper plates and tableware. Instead, they devoured the chicken as they stood in the street, passing police scolding me for blocking traffic. I couldn't help annoying somebody.

ZOOMING WITH MY BROTHER

Light flashed on my computer screen as the young prison guard appeared. "You're here," she said, adjusting the prison camera. "Your brother is right outside the door." It worked - talking by camera through the internet. It was a fad at first, social media for kids with time on their hands.

The pandemic changed everything, computer programs like Zoom carrying out doctor visits, court proceedings, and now, at long last, to reconnect with family. I hated computers, those ghastly devices that swallowed my work. As a window to my soul, the computer had allowed predators to stalk me and steal my identity. On Facebook, someone hijacked my page and changed my name to Harold Washington. I had met and divorced my spouse on the internet.

Now, the computer was helping me heal. He looked good, despite his cancer and weight loss. In our 45 minutes, we talked about family life and the cars we had driven. Peter liked to explain engines, their horsepower and compression, none of which I understood. Nor would I fully understand him, son of the same mother.

The world didn't understand me either, my late-partner Nina pleading to people to, "Make him behave." If nothing else, that's what the pandemic did for me, *"It made me behave, Nina. Yes, it did."*

EPILOGUE

It was sweet seeing life return to normal, kids with big league swagger playing Little League again. At a field not far from my home, I watched 12-year-old Xavier Alcantara step to the plate. His parents were Dominican immigrants, his father, a doctor in the Caribbean, now working in a local fish plant. Now, as friends, they would tell me when their son would be playing athletics. Because of COVID, they had spent a long lock-down year. I sat in the dugout and watched him hit a stand-up double. Rounding the plate, he pumped his fist saying, "That one's for you."

Baseball had not always been so welcoming. Once I had tried umpiring, crouched behind home plate, the ball rocketing toward me. That was unnerving enough. But then, the regular umpire whispered, "You're wearing a cup aren't you?" I needed an explanation. At 50 miles an hour, the baseball could ricochet off the bat, striking me between my legs. I hadn't thought of that, my reproductive organ (or, what was left of it) exposed to peril. With each pitch, I swerved to the side, guessing at balls and strikes. Sometimes I was right, sometimes wrong, as in life itself. That didn't sit well with the fans.

After my stint behind the plate, I walked proudly back to my car. I asked a freckled faced young girl, "How did I do?" Replied the girl, "You suck." Back from the pandemic, I welcomed the chance to "suck" again.